W9-AMO-523

People of the
Ice Age

People of the Ice Age

By RUTH GOODE

Illustrated by DAVID PALLADINI

CROWELL-COLLIER PRESS
Division of Macmillan Publishing Co., Inc.
NEW YORK

Macmillan Publishing Co., Inc., 866 Third Ave., New York, N.Y. 10022
Library of Congress catalog card number: 72–85191
Printed in the United States of America

10   9   8   7   6   5   4   3   2

Library of Congress Cataloging in Publication Data
Goode, Ruth.
    People of the ice age.
    1. Man, Prehistoric—Juvenile literature.   [1. Man, Prehistoric]
I. Palladini, David, illus.   II. Title.
GN743.G65   913′.031   72–85191   ISBN 0–02–736420–8

For Aviva and Jonathan

Contents

People of the Ice Age

Part 1

The Magnificent Hunters

Journey to a Frozen World _____

This story begins with a journey, in its way as strange as a trip to outer space. Getting ready for this journey is not like getting ready for any other kind of trip. Instead of packing things to take along, we can take this journey only if we leave everything behind. We must leave behind not only all things we know, but even the memories of things. Our journey is a trip through time. The world to which we go is a world of very, very long ago, when people had no history and no past and knew none of the things that we know today. It was a wild and beautiful world, but it was also harsh and filled with dangers.

It was a real world, and this is a true story. It is the world's oldest adventure story, the story of the first human beings to live on the earth, how they came to be there, and how they survived.

In that time, nearly half the world was locked in ice. What we know today as a cap of ice, covering the poles and forever frozen, in those days spread right down over the Temperate Zone, nearly halfway to the equator. In places it was a mile thick, a frozen sea as deep as an ocean. It lay over the continents, glittering coldly in sunlight and starlight, silent except for the wild storms that raged across it. It was a world without life.

Into this harsh world came the first people like ourselves to appear on earth. One of their homelands was the southern part of what we know as Europe. To the north spread the unbroken sea of ice. In the heart of the continent, the

Alps towered white under everlasting snows, and from the feet of the mountains another ice sheet spread far into the lowlands all around. The Europe that could support life was hardly more than a shelf of land along the Atlantic and Mediterranean shores.

It was a cold land, a bleak and empty tundra like that of the Arctic today. Gray lichen grew in patches on the bare rocks, and tough grasses found a sparse foothold on the plains. There were no woodlands, no forests, only occasional clumps of ragged shrubs and stunted trees.

In summertime, the edges of the ice sheet melted and sent streams rushing down the valleys, carrying rocks and boulders over the land. In low places the waters spread to form treacherous marshes, and they left great banks of gravel and mud. In the dry season, winds tore at the raw soil and swirled it over the land in yellow dust storms. For thousands of years, the summers were too cool to melt the seas of ice, and the winter snows piled them ever thicker and deeper.

The men who came to live in this world had to share it with some of the largest and fiercest animals in the earth's history. The reindeer, musk ox, elk, and bison that fed on the lichen and the tundra grasses were not dangerous, except in a stampeding herd. But there were also cave bears and cave lions, the huge woolly rhinoceros with two deadly sharp horns thrusting up from its snout, the hairy mammoth like a big humped elephant with enormous tusks spreading in sweeping curves to the sides of its great body. There were ravening wolf packs and scavenging hyenas that would fight fiercely when cornered.

In such a world, how could men survive? They had no
warm coats of fur against the cold, no swiftness like the
deer to escape an enemy, no tusks or fangs for fighting. If
they crept into a cave for shelter, the lion or bear that made
its lair there would tear them to pieces.

Compared with all these splendid, powerful animals, men
were poor, weak things. They were thin-skinned, two-legged,
unarmed against a bitter climate and a host of natural
enemies. They had no history of men who had lived there
before them and from whom they might learn. They had no
books in which they might read what to do.

Houses, cloth for clothing, wagons for carrying, plants
growing in a garden, cows to give milk—all these were still
thousands of years in the future. These men could not
dream or imagine such things. They knew nothing of iron
for tools. They did not even have the useful and friendly
dog or cat to keep them company. They had nothing but
what they could make for themselves with their bare
hands.

Yet they survived. They even made a good life for themselves in this rugged environment. They lived to raise children, and to become our own ancestors. For, like the
fairytale heroes, they had certain remarkable gifts.

Their first gift was that they stood erect, with their
heads held high. They could see over tall grasses and rough,
rocky ground. They could turn their heads to look in all
directions with one swift glance, to track the grazing game
they hunted or to escape the dangerous beasts that hunted
them.

Their second gift was linked to their first, and that was

their two legs. They could not outrun any animal, but they could outwalk them all. They could track the game steadily and patiently for a hundred miles, keeping the beasts moving, keeping them from grazing, until the beasts and not the men were exhausted.

From their upright posture also came their third gift, their arms. The beasts had no arms, only forelegs for running. But men had arms that could bend to many tasks. When they walked, their arms were free to carry and use a weapon, to transport the kill back to camp instead of having to eat their fill on the spot like the animals and then go hungry until the next successful hunt.

Their fourth gift was their hands. The forelegs of the animals ended in hoofs or claws, useful only for running or fighting. But the hands of men had four slender and flexible fingers, and a short, strong thumb that moved opposite to the other four. This meant that men could grasp and hold things. They could pick up a stone and use it as a weapon, a hammer, a cutting tool.

Their fifth gift was their vision. Both their eyes were set at the front of their heads and looked in the same direction. Because of this, they could see in depth. They could judge distances with great accuracy. They could also focus their eyes on an object no more than a foot away and see it sharply and clearly, in every detail.

The sixth and greatest gift was their human brain. The men of this time had brains as large and as fully developed as our own. They could remember experiences of the past and learn from them for the future. They could plan, question, reason. They could figure out ways to do things and to make things, things that would give them protection from the dangers of their world and make the most of their powers and skills.

Their seventh gift was a gift of that intelligent brain. It was the power of speech. Although the beasts also could communicate with each other by voice—most animals have a great variety of calls, signals, and warning cries— only men could speak. Only a man could call to his fellow to bring something, lift something, cut something. Only men could communicate so that they could accomplish difficult tasks together. Only men could tell each other where they had been, what they had seen and done. Only men could teach their children the complicated skills they had learned, could explain to them beforehand about dangers they must avoid. They alone could pass on to the young the wisdom and experience of the old.

These seven gifts stood between the men of the Ice Age and the perils of their harsh world. They were gifts that had come down to them by a slow, natural development that had taken millions of years. There were other creatures that had one or several of these powers, but no creatures on earth had them all, except men.

The first human beings came into the icy world with these powers. The hardships of life in that world challenged their gifts to the utmost, and their minds and skills became sharpened in answer to the challenge. How that came about is the story within the story of our first ancestors.

A World of Slow Time ⎯⎯⎯⎯⎯⎯⎯⎯

In that world of long ago, time moved slowly. We measure the events and eras of that world not in centuries, but in thousands and hundreds of thousands of years. For a hundred thousand years there might be almost no change in the world or the creatures living in it.

The record of the rocks and the seas tells us that the earth began to freeze over nearly a million years ago. By that time the great mountain ranges which had been pushing upward for millions of years, the Alps and the Himalayas, had reached their full height. Their lofty peaks became clothed in snows that never melted, and they acted like giant refrigerators in the centers of the continents, all the while that the ice sheet was spreading out from the North Pole.

For the freezing cycle to begin, the average temperature had to drop only a few degrees. Once it had begun, the ice itself contributed to the cold, and so it kept growing. The northern world became frozen over in this way four separate times in those million and a half years, so that when we speak of the Ice Age we mean a time in the earth's history when there were four successive periods of ice. Each time the ice came, it stayed for fifty or sixty thousand years. Then it melted, and for many thousands of years there would be times of moist, almost tropical warmth. Then the ice came again, and again the northern halves of Europe, Asia, and America were buried under it. The last of the four ages of ice melted away only ten thousand years ago.

And so, during that million and a half years, the Temperate Zone in which we live was sometimes arctic, and sometimes it was so warm and humid that forests and even jungles grew, and jungle animals came to live there. Elephants, hippopotamuses, and saber-toothed tigers lived in Europe and Britain during the warm times.

Seasons of torrential rains came at the end of each warm period and before the coming of the ice. While the ice lay over the northern lands, the Sahara Desert and all the arid northern part of Africa became a lush grassland, teeming with game. When the ice melted, forests grew up in Europe, and the northern African lands became dry and sun-baked as they are today.

As the ice sheets came and went, not only the climate changed. The shape of the land changed as well. Each time the ice formed it sucked up great quantities of the waters of the earth and held them fast in its frozen grasp. The sea level fell, and all around the edges of the continents there was land left high and dry that would otherwise be at the bottom of the sea.

Bridges of dry land reached from Europe at Gibraltar, and from the tip of Italy across Sardinia, right across the Mediterranean to the African shore. The Malaysian peninsula lengthened, and the islands of Indonesia were linked with it and with each other to form one long continuous arm of the continent of Asia, reaching sometimes as far as Australia. Britain was not an island either, but was connected by land across the Dover Straits to northern France.

Each time the ice melted, the oceans filled and these land bridges sank again under the waters. But for long ages during the slow forming and melting of the ice, the men of that time and the animals they hunted moved freely from southern Africa to northern Europe, from the Atlantic and the Mediterranean to the Asian coasts of the far Pacific.

They moved slowly. No one man in his lifetime made his home camp more than a few miles from the place where he was born, even though he might go many miles on a hunt. But little by little, generation after generation, the men of those early times spread all over the livable land of the Old World.

They had plenty of time. The periods of alternate cold and warmth in the Ice Age were almost too long for us to imagine. The first frozen era lasted perhaps one hundred thousand years, and the first warm, or interglacial, period was possibly another hundred thousand years. The second era of ice again lasted about one hundred thousand years, and the warm or interglacial time after that went on for something like two hundred thousand years. The third glacial period was possibly seventy-five thousand years long and the warm time about fifty thousand years. The fourth and last glacier took about sixty thousand years to come and go. And we may be living right now in just another interglacial or warm period between ice eras, with a fifth one still to come. No one knows for certain why the Ice Age began, and so we cannot be sure it has ended.

In all those hundreds of thousands of years of warm interglacial times, men of some kind were living just about everywhere that men now live, except in the far north and in the Western Hemisphere. The Americas also had their Ice Age, with ice sheets even vaster and thicker than in

Europe and Asia, and they had their interglacial warm periods. But if there was human life in those times, the men who lived there left no traces that have yet been discovered.

In Europe, Africa, and Asia, there were men. We know them from fragments of their bones that have been pieced together and from their tools. Some were extremely primitive kinds of men, in the way they looked and the way they lived. Some were more advanced. And some were exactly like ourselves, as we might be if we were born into that kind of world, to make our way with only our inborn human powers.

The Apelike Men

The earliest men of the Ice Age would look very strange to us today. They were about five feet tall, the women a little smaller, and they had almost no forehead and no real chin. If they were hairy—and since all that is left is their bones, we can never really know whether they were—they would look to us like apes that walked upright on two legs. And archeologists first named them *Pithecanthropus erectus*, which is Latin for "erect ape-man." Another name for them is *Homo erectus*, meaning "erect man."

These five-foot, apelike men lived everywhere in the Old World for about half a million years. Their bones have been found in China, Java, Africa, and Europe. A powerful lower jaw discovered near Heidelberg, Germany, and part of a skull and some teeth found in Hungary be-

longed to men like these. The Hungarian fossils are about
five hundred thousand years old, the oldest human remains
found up to now in Europe. Chopping and cutting tools
like theirs, made by chipping stone, have been found in a
valley in Spain, where these men—or men very much like
them—hunted elephants three hundred thousand years
ago.

This early man had a heavy jaw like an ape but his teeth
were more like our own than like ape teeth, only larger. A
thick, bony eyebrow ridge overhung his eyes and ran
straight across the top of his nose, and above it his skull
sloped almost straight back. The bones of his skull were
thick. The size of the space inside it for the brain was
about halfway between an ape's and a modern man's, and
so some scientists have called him the half-brained man.

But in spite of his name and his half-size brain, *Pithecanthropus* was apelike only in looks. In intelligence he
was a man. He did not merely use sticks and stones as apes
and some other animals do. He worked and shaped them
into tools. In his small skull there was already a part of
the brain that controls speech, which even the most intelligent apes do not have. *Pithecanthropus* had some sort of
language. He could teach his children, and he could exchange important information with his fellows.

He walked like a man, on two legs. The great apes are
mainly vegetarians, but this apelike man was a meat-eater
and a mighty hunter. He killed and ate not only deer,
antelope, horses, wild pigs, bison, and water buffalo, but
also elephants, rhinoceros, and even some of the big meat-

eating cats that were his fiercest rivals in the hunt. When the big game were scarce, he ate monkeys, and sometimes he ate his own kind.

In this, too, he was unlike the other animals, which do not ordinarily eat their own kind. Only men have been known to be habitual cannibals, and usually only at certain stages of their development and for special reasons of religious and magical belief. *Pithecanthropus* was apparently a habitual cannibal, at least in those times when he had to be in order not to starve. From the way the bones and skulls in his kitchen refuse are broken open, it is clear that he had a particular taste for the marrow and the brain.

This apelike man conquered the great beasts for his food. He did it not with the teeth and claws and the powerful muscles of his hunting rivals, like the saber-toothed tiger, but with the skills devised by his human brain, small though it was.

Of the many kinds of stones these men found in their various homelands, they chose the kind that could be broken or chipped to form an edge. In China they used quartz and quartzite. In Burma they used petrified wood, as hard as stone but with the grain of wood so that pieces would split off sharply when it was struck. In Europe and Africa they discovered flint such as we too can find in many rocky places in the country.

Flint looks like a dark gray stone but it is a kind of impure glass that occurs in nature. It is as hard as glass and almost as breakable, and its great advantage to the men of long ago was that it chipped or flaked off in pieces with a sharp edge. Through at least half a million years, and perhaps much farther back into the past than that, flint was the principal material from which men made their tools.

Out of a stone or a large pebble that was big enough to fit comfortably in his hand, the apelike man made a chopping tool simply by splitting it and chipping away at one side until he had given it an edge. In the same way, out of a flake of stone, he made a knife. Many stones with natural edges were lying about to be picked up and used. But if a man happened to drop one on a rock, he would notice how neatly it split, and from then on he knew that he could make himself a sharp-edged stone any time he needed one. Most inventions of the past undoubtedly began like this, with an accidental discovery.

Early men had long been accustomed to picking up a stick or a stone in order to club a small, slow-moving animal. The women used sticks to dig up edible roots, to pry open the shell of a tortoise, to turn over a stone and get at the lizards, scorpions, grubs, and such creatures underneath. In hungry times, all these were acceptable food.

But for the real meat of big game, a man needed a weapon he could use from a safe distance. With his stone chopper he could now chop a long straight branch or a sapling. Then with his stone knife he could trim the piece to size and sharpen one end to a point, and he would have a spear.

Some of these men had another great discovery to use. They had fire. A very long time before, men like these had discovered fire when lightning struck and set dry brush or grasses burning, or when a volcano exploded in showers of burning cinders, or sometimes in hot dry weather when a forest went up in flames. The beasts fled in terror from fire. The men were terrified, too, but being men, they were also curious. They went back to the smoldering woods to see what this frightening thing was and what it did.

When they understood that it could keep them warm, protect them from dangerous beasts while they slept, and sharpen the points of their digging sticks, they found ways to take smoldering embers with them and keep the fire alive as well as they could.

Long afterward, perhaps when they were chipping stone for a tool and making the sparks fly, men of a more advanced intelligence learned to make fire for themselves. But it was slow work, harder than keeping alive a fire that they already had. Tending the fire was an important housekeeping task from very early times, and so it remained until quite recently in our own times, until tinderboxes were invented, and then matches. The tinderbox was a great invention, and it is interesting to remember that it contained flint—that very ancient Stone Age material—along with steel to strike a spark.

The apelike man, *Pithecanthropus,* knew how to use a fire, although he did not know how to make one. The remains of his fires of nearly half a million years ago have been found in one of his cave homes in China, near Peking. His fire kept him warm and protected him from night-prowling beasts. Another of its uses was to put a hard sharp point, far sharper than he could cut with his stone knife, on the end of his spear. If a wooden spear was to pierce the hide of an animal, it needed the sharpest possible point. This he could give it by thrusting it into the fire. The tough green wood did not burn, but it charred, and when the charred outer surface was scraped away, the long, slender, hardened point remained.

With such a spear the hunter could lurk far enough away from a grazing herd so as not to disturb it, and at the right moment he could hurl his weapon for the kill. With their stone knives and choppers, he and his fellow hunters in the band would cut up the animal into four or five pieces of a size that a man could carry, and together they would carry their prize back to the camp and their families.

That men could accomplish all this with a wooden spear and a stone knife is not guesswork. It has been seen with modern eyes. When explorers from Europe discovered Tasmania, an island off New Zealand, the people still lived there in the way that men lived half a million years ago, with wooden spears for weapons and chipped stones for tools. The Europeans saw Tasmanian hunters throw their wooden spears a distance of forty yards, to go straight through a hole that was only an inch larger than the thickness of the spear. With such aim and power, it would be nothing remarkable to strike an animal in a vital spot from a similar distance.

To prove the efficiency of stone tools, two Danish scientists once borrowed several Stone Age axes from the Copenhagen Museum and chopped down more than a hundred trees in record time. Those were axes of a later time, and

better made, but still, they were of stone. Natives of a
remote part of central Australia still carve digging sticks,
spears, and even wooden bowls with the same simple kind
of flint knives that *Pithecanthropus* men used to shape
their spears and cut up the meat of their kill.

The Men of the Caves _____

Some time after the second ice sheet spread over the
Northern Hemisphere, the apelike men disappeared from
the earth. Like many kinds of animals in the earth's history
—dinosaurs, saber-toothed tigers, and many more—the
men with small but human brains became extinct.

Even while *Pithecanthropus* still lived on earth, other
kinds of men were living, too. Some of them seem to
have been like *Pithecanthropus*, but of enormous size. We
know them only from some very large teeth that have been
found in China and Java. They were human teeth, but the
men to whom they belonged must have been giants.

Some of the kinds of men who were alive then were more
like ourselves. In the long warm times between the frozen
eras, these different kinds of men moved in small bands
over the Old World, following the game. They made camp
sometimes in the open air, sometimes in rock shelters or in
caves.

There were never many of them at one time, perhaps a
few thousand, spread over a vast area of three continents.
They were different from each other in appearance and in

their stage of development as human beings. Some were already possessed of larger and more highly developed brains than others. They may well have met now and then, and perhaps the men fought each other and took each other's shelters, weapons, and possibly women.

They also learned from each other, and what they principally learned was to improve their tools. The ape-man's crude chopper with a one-sided edge became a well-finished implement, chipped on both sides to make an edge like the edge of an ax. It was an ax without a handle, simply an edged stone held in the fist like the ape-men's choppers, but its double-faced edge was much more efficient.

These hand axes have been found in Africa, the Middle East, and many places in Europe. Some were small, only a few inches long, and some were almost two feet from end to end. Some were skillfully and beautifully finished. The large, handsome axes may not have been used as tools or weapons at all, but rather as symbols of rank or leadership, in the way that a scepter stands for the power of the king.

Unfortunately the people who made and used these hand axes did not leave their fossil bones with their tools, and so we do not know how they looked. But like the *Pithecanthropus* people, they were powerful hunters. They moved back and forth across the land bridges from one continent to another, following the big game. About two hundred and fifty thousand years ago, they and their hand-ax manufacture—whether for tools, weapons, or symbols—disappeared in turn.

Meanwhile, when the third ice sheet melted and the game returned northward into Europe, another kind of men came with it. They may have been descendants of the hand-ax people, because they used some of the same tools. But they made other and better ones.

They made good flint knives, awls with which to bore holes through wood or animal hides, scrapers with which to scrape the hides clean of shreds of flesh and fat so that they could be worn. With a knife they would trim a hide roughly to the shape of clothing, bore holes in it with an awl, and tie it on with strips of hide made into thongs. They also made a new kind of spear, one with a sharpened flint fastened to it as a tip. This was the first time men had figured out how to fit a sharp stone securely to a handle, or haft, and it was a great improvement over the old spear, even with its fire-hardened point.

These were the Neanderthal men. They are called that because their traces were first found in the Neanderthal, a valley in West Germany. But they lived everywhere in Europe and left their records of bones and tools in China, Java, even in South Africa. Some of the most interesting things we know about them we learned from their cave homes and burial places in Palestine and Iraq.

The cartoon or comic-strip drawing of a squat, broad, hairy cave man brandishing a club is supposed to be a picture of a Neanderthal man. This is an old-fashioned version that was based on too little information, some of it quite mistaken. We know much more about these people than was known when Neanderthal remains were first discovered and described, and we now have a much clearer idea of what they were like.

The Neanderthal people were the first creatures on earth to bury their dead with respectful ceremony. The way they did it—putting tools, weapons, and food beside the body—tells us that they believed in a life after death. They were the first people that we know of who tended the old and infirm, and even performed surgical operations to help the maimed. They were the first true cave men, the first we know who stayed in Europe through a time when the ice spread again, braving the cold and hunting the great beasts of that arctic climate.

Although the new men that came after them went far beyond them in their accomplishments, the Neanderthal men were the first people whose ways seem to us especially human.

The Ugly Brave Men _____

The Neanderthal people were far from handsome. They were short and squat, as the cartoons show them, probably no more than five feet, three inches tall. They were strongly built, with heavy bones. Whether they were really hairy we can never know, but it is reasonable to assume that the men did not trim their hair or their beards.

The women did not have combs for their hair, or any aids to grooming or beautifying themselves, and they did not string necklaces of beads or shells, as did all the women who came after them. The men made good tools and weapons for their practical use, but they did not decorate them as the later men did. Theirs was a hard life during the frozen years, and they did not have much time or energy to spare from the struggle to stay alive. They did not take the next step which has seemed so natural to all human beings since their time, the step of becoming interested in beauty, of becoming artists. That remained for the new men, many thousands of years later.

The Neanderthal faces were not much like ours. They still had strong protruding jaws, little chin, the traces of a heavy eyebrow ridge, and a skull that sloped back with almost no forehead. But it was a large skull, wider than the skull of a modern man and deeper at the back, and it contained a brain as large as ours and sometimes even larger, although of a somewhat different shape.

An odd feature was that their arms and legs, although thick and strong, were quite short, especially the forearms below the elbow and the legs from the knee down. Their bodies were also thick and barrel-like. This short, thick stature was an excellent way to be built if one was going to endure severe cold.

Toward the end of the Neanderthal time, their relatives in Palestine were beginning to look somewhat different. We can guess how such a change might come about. Suppose a branch of the family went off to live in Europe, and there the ones that happened to be born taller and thinner did not survive in the bitter climate. But the short, sturdily built ones managed to stay alive and have short, sturdy children like themselves, generation after generation. At the end of thousands of years of separation from the rest of

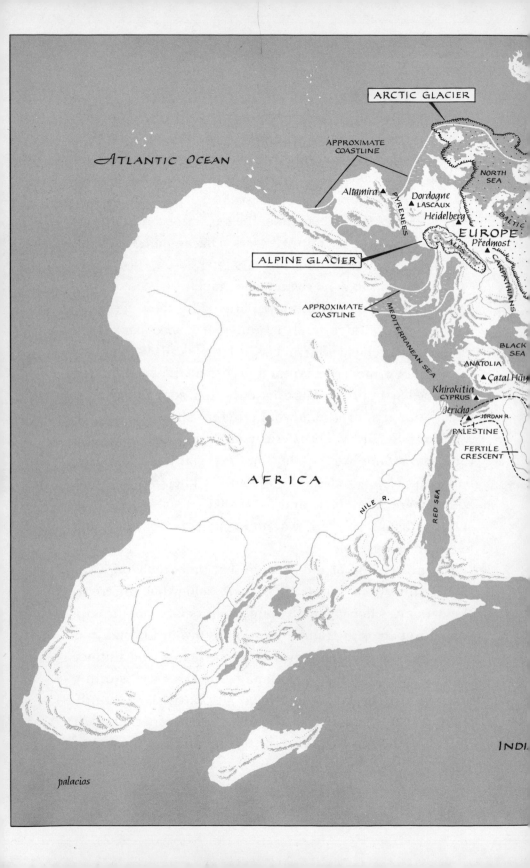

ARCTIC GLACIER

APPROXIMATE
COASTLINE

ATLANTIC OCEAN

NORTH
SEA

Altamira ▲

Dordogne
▲ LASCAUX

Heidelberg ▲

BALTIC

EUROPE

ALPS

Předmost ▲

CARPATHIANS

ALPINE GLACIER

PYRENEES

APPROXIMATE
COASTLINE

MEDITERRANEAN SEA

BLACK
SEA

ANATOLIA

▲ Çatal Hü...

Khirokitia
CYPRUS ▲

Jericho ▲

JORDAN R.

PALESTINE

FERTILE
CRESCENT

AFRICA

NILE R.

RED SEA

INDI...

palacias

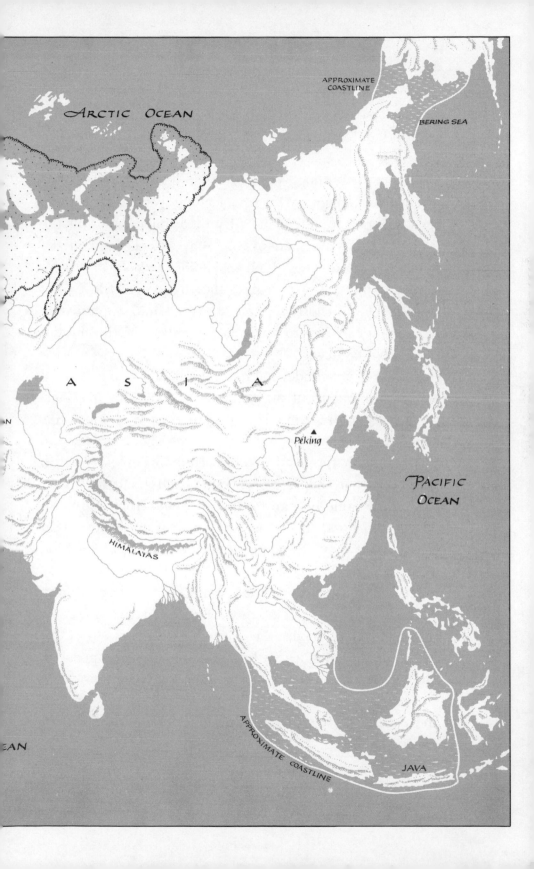

ARCTIC OCEAN

APPROXIMATE
COASTLINE

BERING SEA

A   S   I   A

▲
Péking

PACIFIC
OCEAN

HIMALAIAS

APPROXIMATE COASTLINE

JAVA

their people, the European branch of the family would look very different from their relations in warmer parts of the world.

That is pretty much what seems to have happened. The Neanderthal people were the leading people of Europe for about one hundred and fifty thousand years, and the last sixty thousand years of their stay was the time of the fourth ice era, during which they had Europe all to themselves. At the end of that time they had very little family resemblance to those of their kind that had remained in Palestine, or in fact to any other members of the human family, old or new.

And yet if a Neanderthal man in a business suit, shaved and with his hair cut, were to stand next to us in a bus, we would not give him a second glance. He would look like an ordinary man who happened to be short, broad, and without much forehead or chin. Human beings come in many different shapes and sizes, and although we all belong to the same human family, we come from many different ancestors. There is good reason to believe that Neanderthal men, or some branch of the Neanderthals, were among our ancestors.

The life of the Neanderthals in Europe was easy at first, in the warm interglacial time. But when the ice came again, the plant foods, the fruits and berries and edible roots, and the small, easily hunted animals all disappeared. Through the bitter years of the fourth glacier, these men hunted the mammoth and the woolly rhinoceros for food and fought the cave bears and the cave lions for their shelters.

They were fine spearsmen, and their flint-tipped spears were the best that men had made up to that time. To trap the great beasts, they would dig a pitfall, a deep hole lined with sharp wooden stakes fixed into the sides and pointing upward, to pierce an animal's body as it fell. To hunt the herds of reindeer and horses, they went out in companies of men, carrying flaming brands. Shouting and flourishing their fiery torches, they would stampede a herd over a cliff, then finish off the injured animals at its foot with clubs. There are cliffs in Europe with thousands of animal bones below them, in layers that tell us the cliff was used in this way for thousands of years.

Still it was hard to stay alive in that world, and few people lived to be more than thirty years old. Many babies did not survive, and many people died of the cold or of illness. Many were killed by animals or perished in accidents. Even a minor injury could be fatal. If a hunter merely sprained an ankle when he was far from the home cave, or if he suffered a wound and became too weak to walk from loss of blood, his companions would have to abandon him or else all of them might freeze to death. And the families waiting at home would die, too—of starvation.

There were accidents in the caves as well. One such accident left its traces for explorers of our own time to find, and it tells a remarkable story. It tells us that despite the hard life they lived, the Neanderthal people cared for each other when they could. This was a cave in which the roof fell in and killed the entire family of ten that was living there.

There were children, young men and women, and one old man. One of the younger men had only one arm. The other arm may have been crippled from birth or it may have suffered an injury, for it had been neatly and successfully amputated at the elbow. The old man was about fifty. His joints were so swollen with arthritis that he could scarcely have walked a step, and he had lost all his teeth. But his people had looked after him, had brought him food, and must have even chewed the tough raw meat for him. They had kept him alive until a single accident killed them all and left the record for us to read.

That family was found lying where they had died, in one of the Neanderthal cave homes in Palestine. Another cave in that part of the world tells another remarkable story of the kind of people those Neanderthals were, despite their brutish looks. Here, a man was ceremoniously laid to rest after he had died, perhaps also in an accident since his skull was badly crushed. He was a strong man, tall for a Neanderthal—five feet eight inches, or about the height of a medium-sized modern man. What is astonishing about this man is that he was buried on a bed of flowers.

On that spring day when he died, sixty thousand years ago, some people who had loved or revered him had clambered over the hillsides and gathered armfuls of wild flowers. They had cut evergreen boughs and had spread and twined the flowers among the green foliage to make a bright and fragrant bed for this man whose death they mourned. From the pollens that still remained of this flowery litter, we know that they were small, brightly colored spring blossoms, ancient relatives of our modern grape hyacinths, bachelor's-buttons, hollyhocks, and yellow groundsel.

This discovery was made in 1960, in a cave in the Zagros Mountains along the border between Iran and Iraq. Today the hillsides around the cave are dry and barren, but sixty thousand years ago they were covered with pine forests and flowering meadows. At that time, Europe lay frozen under its fourth ice cap, and the European branch of the Neanderthal family was hunting the giant Ice Age beasts and learning to stay alive in arctic cold. They did not have flowers to bury their dead. But they laid them carefully to rest in the postures of sleep, and they spread over the bodies handfuls of red, ocherous earth, perhaps in the magic belief that this earth, with its color of life, would restore the dead to life in some afterworld.

The Neanderthals learned many skills that helped them to keep alive in a frozen world, but they did not learn quite enough. They may not have cooked their food, and they may not have known how to make a fire. The meat of game animals, eaten raw or even half raw, meant long hours spent chewing and eating in order to get enough nourishment, for the Neanderthals had human jaws and teeth, not like those of the flesh-eating beasts. That meant fewer hours for rest, for making tools and weapons, for thinking and planning. And if the fire went out, and if there was no nearby camp where they could get some live embers to start another, the whole family could perish.

The skills of making fires and cooking food remained for the new men to learn. The fourth ice cap was melting and the last frozen period of the Ice Age was coming to an end when these new men appeared.

At the same time, the Neanderthal people vanished. What happened to them is one of the unsolved mysteries of that long-past time.

Their European homeland was still an arctic world, even though it was slowly warming. There were probably never more than about two thousand of the Neanderthal people, living in small, scattered bands. Did some of them lose their fire and perish in the cold? Did an epidemic of illness wipe some of them out? Did the hardships of their life kill so many that too few strong men remained for the hunting, and too few women to bear and raise children?

Did they meet the new men, fight for their homes and hunting grounds, and lose all, together with their lives? Did they mingle and intermarry with the new people and so become part of the future after all?

All these things may have happened. The European Neanderthals vanished, but the Middle Eastern branch of the family did develop something of the new faces and bodies of the new kind of men, whether by intermarriage or through evolutionary change.

How the Neanderthals' story ended we may never know. But they left their record as part of the story of man, a people of homely looks but with some of the human qualities that we most admire. They were courageous, inventive, and capable of treating each other with respect and tenderness.

The New Men _____

People with high foreheads, full-sized brains, and well-formed chins seem to have lived in Europe now and then during the warm periods. Some scientists believe that they existed all through the Ice Age, following the warm weather north and going south again when the ice returned. If they did, they left only very little trace of themselves, and their toolmaking skills were no different from those of other people of the times.

Now the time was about forty thousand years ago. The ice was melting, although it would return again and again in the next several thousand years, for shorter periods each time, but yet long enough to test the powers of the new people.

They were a tall people, up to six feet and sometimes taller, with long legs and long, strong, well-built bodies. Their faces were like ours, with shapely chins and no protrusion of the jaws. Their eyebrows lay flat above the eyes, with almost no bony ridge, and they had foreheads like our own. Their skulls were in every way like ours, arched over the top and rounded at the back to meet a long, slender neck.

They are called the Cro-Magnon men from the name of the cave in southern France where the first fossils of their bones were found. They are also called *Homo sapiens*, "knowing man" or intelligent man. And that is our own name, and the name of all human beings living today. Whatever the color of our skin, our kind of eyes or hair, or the size and shape of our bodies, wherever and however we may live, that is our species name and we are all members of the one human species.

The Cro-Magnon people may not have been the first of our species in the world. A few earlier skulls or parts of skulls have been found that are like the *Homo sapiens* skull in shape, although the bone is much thicker. One of these was discovered at Swanscombe in England, another at Fontéchevade in France, and a few elsewhere.

All of them date from warm periods before the fourth era of the ice. But none of these previous ancestors seem to have braved the hard life of ice-covered Europe. Unlike the Neanderthal men, these early men of our modern species apparently fled to warmer lands where the life was easier. There, with little challenge and a great deal of time, they slowly perfected their human powers.

When the Cro-Magnon people appeared in France between forty thousand and thirty-five thousand years ago, they were in full possession of all the seven gifts of man. They were the ones that remained when all the others, including the earlier men of their own kind, had disappeared. The Cro-Magnon men and the men that came after them flourished and peopled the earth.

Before we go on to see how they did this, we must answer a question that has hovered over all our story so far. How did they come to have these human powers? How did the seven gifts of man come to be?

Part 2

How Men Began

Overleaf:
About two million years ago in South Africa, a nearly human family of small, erect creatures may have lived like this under a rock shelter. A mother nurses her baby, a youth drinks water from a spring in the rock, and others are at work chipping stone for rough weapons.

The Seven Gifts

These were the seven gifts that made human beings different from all other creatures on earth: the upright posture, the long-striding walk, the free-moving arms, the five-fingered hands, the eyes that looked forward, the thinking and reasoning brain, the power of speech. To see how they came to be, we must leave the Ice Age and turn the world a long way back, some thirty million years into the past.

The earth of thirty million years ago was already a green garden, with most of the plants that we know today already growing in it. There were bushes and vines with berries on them, trees with nourishing nuts and fruits, wild grains, roots, stems, and leaves that could be eaten.

The huge reptiles, the dinosaurs, had vanished perhaps seventy million years before. Little warm-blooded mammals that had lurked under the giant tree-ferns and kept out of the way of the dinosaurs had succeeded in outlasting them. These little creatures, no bigger than our squirrels, had branched out into many families. The wolf-dogs, the big cats, the wild pigs rooting with their tusks, and the grass-eating ancestors of deer, elephants, horses, cattle—all had appeared on the earth of thirty million years ago.

Fish swam in the seas and birds flew in the air. One of the warm-blooded animal families lived in the trees and ate the fruits that grew there. These were the monkeys, the first members of the primate family.

The monkeys in the trees did not develop hoofs like the grass-eaters, nor paws like the wolf-dogs, nor claws like the

cats. They kept unchanged the little five-fingered feet that
they had inherited from the ancient reptiles. You can still
see such feet on small lizards today. The monkeys used
these feet like hands, to grasp the branches as they swung
along in the trees and to pick the fruits that were their
food.

Unlike some other animals, the monkeys had flat faces
and both their eyes were placed at the front of their heads
instead of one on each side of a protruding nose. Both of
their eyes looked straight ahead, in the same direction,
and both saw the same object. But because the eyes were
some distance apart, each eye saw a little farther around
the object on its own side. When the two images, one from
each eye, came together in the brain, the picture was not
flat like a picture but in the round as the object actually
was. The monkeys saw things in three dimensions, as we
do.

This was a great help in judging distances when they
swung from branch to branch. And they developed a habit
of chattering and calling to each other across the treeways.
Such a habit is not safe on the ground where bigger animals lurk, but it is necessary in the trees where they could
not always see their fellows through the thick leaves. Birds,
too, are very talkative, always chattering, twittering, calling, and singing.

About thirty million years ago, a new kind of primate
appeared that was much larger and stronger than the monkeys and was able to live on the ground. It may be that the
trees were thinning out at that time as a result of changes
in climate. It takes only a little less rainfall each year to

transform a thick woodland into a treeless, grassy plain over a period of years. Or it may be that the new kind of primates were just too big and heavy to live in the trees. Other species have changed their size dramatically at certain stages of their development. The little dawn-horse, the ancestor of our horse, was no bigger than a dog.

We know about the large, ground-dwelling primate only from its fossil bones, because it became extinct on earth a long time ago.

This early ape lived on the ground and had to compete for food with the big beasts that also lived there, the meat-eating cats and wolf-dogs. It had to defend itself, too, from these hunting animals. And it already had some important advantages over these other animals.

It had the free-moving arms and five-fingered hands of its tree-dwelling monkey cousins. It had their kind of vision, and it had their voices. It also had a special kind of brain, which depended not on the sense of smell like the other animals on the ground, but on its vision.

We must stop for a moment to look into this. How does a brain grow?

Hand, Eye, Brain _____

Think of the brain as a center of communications, a telephone switchboard no larger than a tiny transistor but more complicated than a giant computer. The nerves come into it like long telephone lines from all the sense organs— eyes, nose, ears, the tiny organs of touch, cold, warm, wet, dry in every square inch of the skin, the sense organs in the muscles that send messages when we are moving, pushing, lifting. The nerves bringing these messages are the sensory nerves. And another set of nerves, the motor nerves, goes out to the muscles. The brain receives information by way of the sensory nerves, and on the basis of that information it sends out instructions along the motor nerves to the muscles: Go this way, not that way; stand up, crouch down, run; watch out, danger, hide; here's ripe fruit, pick it, eat it.

When a part of the brain works particularly hard it grows and becomes able to do more and more. In this respect the brain is like the muscles, lungs, or any other part of the body. We all develop our brains by using them.

The ground animals get most of their information from their noses. Your dog is color-blind and quite near-sighted, but with his sense of smell he can find you in a crowd without the least trouble. All ground animals have a far more developed sense of smell than we do, and so they have what is called a "nose brain"—a large, especially well-developed part of the brain that sends out its instructions on the information that it gets from the animal's sense of smell.

But the little animals that went to live in the trees could not get along up there, far above the ground, on their sense of smell. They needed to see. And so in the course of many, many generations of change, they developed an "eye brain," which controls most of their actions by what they see. Birds and monkeys share this well-developed part of the brain for sight.

Something else was also encouraging the brain to grow, and that was the five-fingered hand. Compare a hand with a hoof, a paw, or a claw, and you will quickly see how a hand needs much more complicated muscle and nerve connections.

A hoof is nothing but a big, specially developed finger-nail, hard and thick but without much sensation and without any muscle. A dog's paw has sensitive pads like the sole of your foot, but it cannot move the individual pads any more than you can move your individual toes, perhaps not as much. A cat's paw has claws that can be thrust out for climbing, or for scratching in attack or defense, and so each pad provides muscular control for a claw. But again, a cat cannot push out one claw and keep the rest sheathed. All the claws of the foot come out together, or they are all withdrawn and sheathed together.

But the five fingers of a hand can each move separately from the others. Not all are equally independent, to be sure. The fourth and little fingers move together most of the time. But even those fingers can learn to move separately, and they do when we are playing the piano or touch-typing on the typewriter. The individual muscles and nerves are there to be used.

A monkey has just such a hand. A monkey's hand is equipped to do just about everything a human hand can do. The difference is that the monkey's brain is not equipped to direct and use it. For the life in the trees, the monkey brain developed as far as it needed to go.

On the ground, the ape branch of the family developed quite a bit further, especially the chimpanzees and the orangutans. A chimpanzee named Viki was brought up by human parents with their little boy of about the same age, and she learned to do almost everything a bright three-year-old child can do. What is more, she learned those things at a much younger age than a human child. Her muscular strength and control for climbing, jumping, and even using her hands came much sooner. But three-year-old skills turned out to be the limit of her learning.

The newest branch of the primate family did not stop there. The brain that was to become a human power went on growing, through one stage after another, in creatures that were more and more human. The hand with its five independent, flexible fingers, the eyes with their sharp and accurate vision, pushed and pulled the intelligence into all kinds of new efforts, into trying all kinds of new actions and practicing to gain skill in those that proved useful. All this took thousand of generations, millions and billions of repetitions, and many generations that made no progress at all.

Every time a new action was performed, it meant that a new nerve connection was made, or rather a whole series of new connections, or nerve pathways. And each time this happened, a part of the brain developed to manage the communications of sensory nerves and motor nerves in order to control the new combinations.

A first step in such a new development came when an ape or an ape-man picked up a stone or a stick and used it. And a second and greater step came when he discovered a way to change the stick or the stone, to make it into a better tool or weapon.

When hands and eyes began to work closely together to make something—to chip a stone for a cutting edge, to carve a stick to a digging point or a spear point—then the primate brain was on the way to full human growth, with all its remarkable powers of inventing and learning. When he became a toolmaker, the ancestral primate became a man.

The Human Family _____

With this great step came another, the birth of the human family. Other animals live in families while the children are young and need to be cared for, and if you have ever watched a mother cat teach her kittens, you know that human parents did not invent the education of the young. The difference is that human children take so much longer to learn. This is not because they are less bright than the children of other species, but because they have so very much more to learn.

Most of what the other animal children have to learn is already built into their brains at birth, and it needs only to be developed by experience. We say that most of what a cat does is instinctive, meaning that it is born into the cat brain. Only a rather small part of the brain is for learning things that are altogether new in the life of cats.

In the human brain, a very large part has been developed that is just for inventing and learning things that are new in the life of human beings. The power to learn is inborn, but not the thing learned.

This kind of learning takes a long time. The monkey child or the ape child quickly reaches its full powers and is able to look after itself in its natural environment. But the new primate child, with its great possibilities of growth and learning, took a much longer time. Instead of months, like a monkey, or a year or so, like an ape, the human child took years to learn what danger was and how to escape it. He took even longer to be able to manage food, shelter, fire, the art of making and using tools, and the very special human skills of hunting.

The human child needed grownups, or at least older children, to look after it through that long time. And so the human family was born, of parents and grandparents, uncles and aunts, brothers and sisters and cousins, all living and working together, looking after the children and helping each other.

A new emotion was born, too, the emotion of love that members of a family have for each other, and which they keep their whole lives long. Animals show love of this kind when they live with human beings. A pet dog or cat is attached to its human family, and suffers when it is separated from them. Some animals in nature live in groups— a pack of wolves, a pride of lions, a horde of monkeys—and they are attached to the members of their own group and wary of outsiders. And animal parents surely show as much love for their young as human parents do for their children. But it is unlikely that a lion cub knows its own mother when it is grown up. Human love, the life-long attachment to certain other human beings, was a new thing in the world.

Learning to Talk _____

Out of this new way of living grew still another power,
one that no other creature ever possessed or ever seemed to
need. That was the power of speech.

The monkeys in the trees were noisy chatterers. They
had learned to use their voices and had begun to develop
a special part of the brain for it. The structure of the
throat changed, too, making their chatter so easy and natural that they could rattle on all day without effort and stop
babbling only to eat and sleep. All this was ready when
the early ape took to living on the ground.

In the apes this power never developed any further. We
mentioned Viki, the chimpazee that learned to do most of
the things a human child of three could dc. But Viki never
went beyond a one-year-old in learning to speak. Her
human parents worked with her for long hours, and in the
end she learned to say only four words: "mama," "papa,"
"cup," and "tsk," which meant cigarette.

Human babies begin practicing to talk by the time they
are three months old. They coo and babble, playing with
sounds in the same way that they will hold up a hand and
play at wriggling their fingers. No animal child of any
species plays at making sounds. Viki could not learn to talk
because only the human brain has a special area developed
for speech. Parrots and parakeets, myna birds, and some
other kinds of birds learn to mimic speech, but they do not
really talk. They are not able to tell us anything, only to
make sounds they have already heard.

We can see how the power of speech had to be born.

The human family, living and working together, needed to talk to each other. A father teaching his son how to track a deer, or make a spear, or chip flint for a knife would need some words to tell him. A mother sending the children out to gather food or wood would need words to tell them what she wanted, where to go for it, how much to bring, what to watch out for on the way. This was an altogether different kind of teaching from what the mother cat teaches her kittens. Only some of it could be acted out. The power of speech gave human beings an enormous advantage in teaching and learning.

We will never know for certain what men's first words were. We read in the Bible how the Lord brought all the animals to Adam and he named them, and perhaps the first words were names for things. Some of the scientists believe that the first words were not names but actions, or rather requests for actions.

In that world, men often had to do things together that were too difficult for one man to do alone. Men working together at a complicated job, like digging a pitfall to catch a mammoth, needed words that would be quite specific: Lift this, bring that, chop this. If a man was injured or in danger, he might just call out for help. But if a hunter had a dangerous animal cornered, he would not simply call for help. He would want to tell his fellows which way to approach and how to kill the beast without getting him or themselves killed or injured in the process.

Once men learned to talk, they opened the doors to a marvelous new world of the mind, a world of memory and imagination, of history and storytelling, of poetry and legend, science and religion. Now a man could tell about things that had happened in another time and place, to himself or to other men. Parents could tell their sons and daughters what their own parents had told them, and so the knowledge of the past could be handed down. People could discuss what might happen, and what should be done about it, and so planning for the future became possible.

Some very important practical skills could develop only by the use of words, for example the commonplace skill of learning to count. A crow, a very intelligent bird, can count up to six or seven. So can a pigeon. So can a human being, if a number of objects are flashed before him on a screen too quickly for him to count them in words. Without words for the numbers, a man can count no higher than the birds, except if he uses his fingers, and then he can count at least up to ten. But without words he soon reaches a point at which he loses count, and he can only say that there are "many."

With words, men could begin to think and reason, to figure out cause and effect, to look for explanations of the mysterious events in nature. They could seek meanings in the things that happened, like storms and accidents and a scarcity of game, and they could try to control the happenings that affected their lives and well-being. Out of this came religious belief and ritual, and later scientific theory and experiment.

Men probably learned to talk, at least in the simplest ways, at about the time that they began to make tools and to learn the use of fire. From then on, the powers of hands, eyes, and language, all working together, quickened the astonishing development of the human brain.

The Inborn Changes

We must not imagine that the new powers were learned by individual human beings in the course of living, in the way that we learn from babyhood to walk and talk and make use of our hands. When we learn these skills, we are only learning to make use of powers that already exist in our brains and nerves and muscles. Our capabilities are born in us as human beings. But they are there because they came to exist in the first place by a natural process, the process of natural selection. We have to understand how this works.

In any family, the children are more like their brothers and sisters, and more like their parents and grandparents, than they are like other children and parents and grandparents. But they are also different from each other in a great many ways. Each child has his or her individual characteristics.

In our human world, it does not matter very much if a child is shorter or taller or has good vision or strong muscles or can run fast. If his eyes are not so good he can have glasses. If he is not big enough to play football he can play other games. If he is not very muscular he may not be a good athlete, but there are other things he can do well.

None of these individual characteristics makes too much difference. If he cannot develop one skill, he can develop another.

But in nature the competition is fiercer. An individual trait may be an advantage in one kind of environment and a disadvantage in another, and in some situations it may mean the difference between life and death.

So, living in the trees, a monkey that had a good sense of smell but not very good eyesight might fall to its death by missing a branch. Or, if it did not perish suddenly by accident, it still might not do very well in the competition for food. The monkey with sharper eyesight would make its way safely and swiftly along the treeways, and get the most and the best fruits. It would grow strong, and live long, and have many children. Some of its children would inherit its good eyesight, and they, too, would do well in the life of the trees.

When we speak of monkeys having good eyesight, we are not speaking just of good distance vision. We are speaking of good sharp vision of objects close by. A monkey had to be able to judge whether a nearby branch was exactly within reach on its next swing. And just as important, it had to be able to see whether the branch was unoccupied, or whether there was perhaps a snake lurking there, coiled and waiting to strike. A snake could lie utterly still, nearly invisible in the dappled light that came through the leaves. And the snake was the one deadly enemy of the monkeys in the trees.

A monkey also had to see an object very close, such as a

piece of fruit held in its hand. Was it ripe for eating? Did it have bad spots, spoiled spots? And in order to be eaten with the monkey's small, almost human teeth, certain fruits had to be peeled.

For this kind of seeing, whether of the branch, the snake, or the fruit, the monkey has its eyes set at the front of its head, both able to focus on the same nearby object. We call this stereoscopic vision, meaning that two images, one from each eye, are superimposed to form one image. This is the same principle as in a stereo phonograph, which has two speakers placed in different parts of the room, or a stereo recording, which is made with two or more microphones in different places in the studio. To see stereoscopically means to see that an object is not just a flat surface but has sides—it is solid. And that means seeing in depth.

In the early days of the little primates in the trees, one of them may have been born with eyes set closer together toward the front of its face. This would be one of the inborn, individual differences that can occur, and we call such inborn differences mutations. If a monkey was born with such a mutation, with its eyes set far enough forward so that it had stereoscopic vision, then that monkey would have an advantage. And so would those among its children that inherited this forward position of the eyes. And in many generations, a race of monkeys would grow up that had a very substantial advantage for the life in the trees.

The gift of walking came slowly, from crouching ape to erect two-legged man with his hands free for carrying and fighting. Feet, legs, pelvis, spine, and head position all changed.

That is what is meant by natural selection. Natural selection is the first and most important principle of the theory of evolution. What it means is that the natural environment does the selecting. In the struggle for existence in nature, those creatures that are best fitted for their environment are the ones that will survive. And if an animal happens to be born with an especially good new trait, one that gives him an advantage in the competition for food, safety, and good living space, that animal is likely to thrive.

That animal is also likely to have many children, and gradually its children with the advantage will push the less gifted animals out of the best places. And those children will pass on their new inborn trait, their lucky mutation, to their children, and they will thrive and perhaps even improve on the gift that their ancestor has handed down to them.

Great Ape on the Ground _____

Mutations happen all the time, and most of them are not important one way or the other. But there are times when a mutation is of the utmost importance. That is when an animal finds itself in a new environment, or when the environment in which it has been living undergoes some change. Then the species must either adapt its old powers to the new environment, or it must enjoy some lucky mutations and give rise to a new species with new powers.

On the grassy plains where he now lived, the early ape already had one lucky mutation. He was several times as large as his monkey cousins in the trees, and among the big animals on the ground his size was an advantage.

But he also had to adapt the tree skills of his primate family to ground skills. Without the ground animals' keen sense of smell to guide him, he had to make the best use of his good eyesight. He had to be able to stand upright and look around.

Suppose we look again at this matter of arms and legs. In their tree life, swinging from branch to branch, the little primates developed forelegs and hind legs that could move independently.

If you watch a dog or a horse running, you will see that its forelegs and hind legs move in rhythm with each other. When a horse walks or trots, its legs alternate, the right foreleg stepping forward at the same time as the left hind leg, and the left foreleg with the right hind leg. When it gallops, the forelegs go forward together as a pair, and then the hind legs as a pair. Only very specially trained horses, like the dancing horses in the circus, can change this pattern and move their legs independently to some extent.

A horse can kick out with one hind leg, or paw the ground with one front hoof. The other quadrupeds also have some independent action in their legs. A dog can scratch itself with its hind foot. A cat has very special motions with its front paws when it washes its ears and whiskers. Some other animals, such as squirrels and otters, use their front paws almost like hands for eating. But none of them has the really free-acting forelegs that we would call a pair of arms.

The primates developed these free-moving arms in the
trees. They could move their legs in rhythm like the quadrupeds when they ran along on all fours. But they could
also move a foreleg independently to reach and get hold of
a branch. Some of them developed a tail, a kind of fifth
leg, which also could reach and wind around a branch. The
monkeys also developed a habit of sitting upright (as does
the squirrel, another tree animal). When all these mutations were put together, a new race of monkeys was born.
They could reach out an arm to pick a fruit, sit and peel
it with their clever little hands, and pop it into their
mouths. Watch them do it the next time you go to the zoo.
The lion holds his food down with his great paws and tears
at it with his teeth. But the monkey sits and eats daintily,
putting food into its mouth with its hands.

On the ground, the early ape found good use for these
arms and hands. He could pick up a stick or a rock and
use it as a weapon, as his descendants in the ape family all
do. The forest apes also use their arms to hoist themselves
into the trees for safe sleeping at night. Apes that live in
rocky or mountainous country, like the baboons and the
Barbary apes, use their arms and legs for climbing, much
like the monkeys in the trees.

But the early ape lived on the plains, amid high grass,
and he had neither trees nor rocks to climb. Down on all
fours, he could not see the game or the enemy. The lion
could track him with its nose, but he could not track the
lion unless he could see it. And so he had to learn not
only to stand up on his two hind legs, but to walk on them.

Walking, the Great Mutation _____

On the ground, the early ape learned to walk upright. This was a tremendous change, as great as the one the birds undertook when they learned to fly. And it involved a mutation as great as the mutation of growing wings.

Walking demanded feet that were broad and strong enough to support the body's whole weight. It required longer, stronger legs. It needed a kind of spine and bony structure that could hold the body upright. It needed new nerve and muscle combinations to balance the body.

These enormous changes did not come all at once. Some of them did not come at all to the early ape, nor to many of his descendants. The great apes that we know today can stand erect and they can walk a few steps, but when they really want to travel they get down and lope along on three or four legs, using the knuckles of one or both hands on the ground. And a chimpanzee's feet are still more like hands than like human feet.

It took many successive mutations and many different species to make all the necessary changes for a genuine two-legged, walking stride. One of the most important mutations was in the spine, which evolved from the arched back of a quadruped to the double-curved shape, like the letter S, of our own spine. The double curves make it possible to support considerable weight on a slender, flexible rod that is held upright.

The human foot has two springy arches, too. One is under the instep and a smaller one, called the metatarsal arch, is built into the front of the foot just before the toes. The human foot also has a heel bone, another mutation. And the toes were still another mutation: a change from long, grasping fingers to short, supporting toes.

The bony girdle of the hips, which we call the pelvis, had to change its shape and become strong enough to hold the trunk erect and give freedom to the legs. The great apes have powerful shoulders; but, like the four-legged animals, they have a small and narrow pelvis compared with man's. The wide, strong human pelvis was a most important change in the body structure, and it came next to last in the stages of human development.

Last to come was the position of the head on top of the spine. In the apes, as in the four-legged animals, the head is set forward as though the top of the spine went straight up along the back of the skull. But in man, the head is just about centered on the neck, and this adds greatly to ease and balance in walking.

Incidentally, the position of the head was an addition to his use of his good eyesight, because he could turn and bend his head in just about any direction—up, down, and to the sides. In the same way, his flexible spine became an addition to the use of his hands, because he could bend forward, to the sides, and even twist around to the back, thus extending the reach of his arms.

All in all, once these many changes had been accomplished, the walking man was truly a marvelous creature. As a form of locomotion, his was more remarkable than anything in nature except the flight of a bird.

The Meat-Eaters _____

The early ape made another adaptation on the ground. He learned to eat meat.

In the trees the primates were all vegetarians, except for occasionally robbing a bird's nest for the eggs or the fledgling birds. The apes are still vegetarians. The gorillas, for all their size and ferocious appearance, eat only plant foods, and they have to eat almost all day long, like the cattle and sheep and deer, in order to nourish their powerful bodies.

All the original ape's descendants in the ape line are vegetarians. They have big chewing teeth, and some of them have canines, or eyeteeth, that are long sharp fangs, used for shredding the coarse leaves and stems that they eat and as dangerous weapons in fighting.

But the big original ape became omnivorous, meaning that he ate everything. He could not pounce on the deer and other big game, as the great cats could. He could not harry the game to death as the wolves hunting in packs could do. He had to be content with the small, slow-moving game which he could catch with his hands or kill with a rock. Still, he did well enough to father a whole new branch of primates before he himself became extinct.

Much, much later the meat-eating habits that came from the first ground ape encouraged his new descendants to become skillful hunters, able to compete with the lions and tigers and even to hunt them. Meanwhile, every one of these changes, every new use of hands and eyes, every advance in standing and walking, in tracking and capturing new kinds of game, made new demands on the intelligence. The brain grew, and it continued to grow with each new species of the primate family.

The New Line of Primates _____

The first descendants we know about in the new primate line left their fossil bones in southern Africa about two million years ago. They were small creatures about the size of a chimpanzee, and they weighed between fifty and eighty pounds.

They had small teeth, very like human teeth. They walked upright, although they did not yet have the completely new pelvic structure that would allow the long, untiring strides of a walking man. And they already had a brain that was large in proportion to their small bodies, larger than the brain of an ape of the same size.

They also had the latest structural mutation for walking, the head centrally placed at the top of the spine. With this change, their small teeth, and the upright, two-legged walk, they were no longer true apes, although they were not quite human either. Because their traces were found in South Africa they are called *Australopithecus*, meaning "southern ape."

From the same or a similar branch of the ape family came another man-ape, also African. This one was just about twice the size of *Australopithecus*, or as big as men

are today, but his brain was no larger than that of the little
southern ape in proportion to his size. Still, he was intelligent enough to use large, pebble-shaped stones as tools
and weapons, and his kind of manlike ape spread to many
parts of Africa and possibly all the way to Java. He is called
Paranthropus, meaning "nearly man."

Now this kind of primate had reached human size, an
advantage in living among the big animals of the plains.
He had learned to use a stone as a tool or a weapon to
help him get his food and to defend himself against animals bigger, swifter, and much better equipped for hunting and fighting than he was. The challenge of living on
the ground, of having to make the most of his hands and
eyes and upright posture in competition with the fierce
hunting animals of his world, had already had an effect
on the growth of his brain.

From this point on, the brainiest primate children were
the ones that would flourish in the world. For now the
world was changing.

For millions of years, the earth forces had been quiet,
and the creatures of the earth could wander in a green
garden full of fruits for the picking, like what we think of
as the Garden of Eden. The climate over most of the world
was sometimes a little warmer or a little cooler, sometimes
rainy and sometimes dry, but generally the weather was
mild. There were forests and there were broad grassy
plains, and each of the many kinds of animal found its
own environment, the one for which it was best suited.

Now this Edenlike time was ending. In the middle of

Europe and Asia, great mountains were thrusting up from the crust of the earth. Presently the earth turned cold and colder, and the ice came.

Hearth Fire and Cave Home

Now the challenge of changing environments came faster, not in millions but in hundreds of thousands of years, and then in thousands. The man-apes vanished, and the ape-men, the *Pithecanthropus* men, managed to survive a little longer. Some of them learned two most important additions to their way of life. They learned to use fire, and they learned to make their homes in caves. Men like them, or perhaps men who were something between the *Pithecanthropus* and the sturdy Neanderthal men, had hearth fires in Europe seven hundred and fifty thousand years ago.

It was probably the cold that prompted them to bring embers from some natural fire, like a burning forest or a volcanic eruption, and build a fire in the mouth of the cave. They discovered that with fire they could chase the cave lions or cave bears out of a good cave and keep it for themselves. They used fire to drive the animals in a hunt, to keep the animals away when they rested, and to sharpen their spears.

But the wonder of fire was more than keeping warm in a freezing world, more than a new and miraculous weapon in the hunt or a practical help in making a good spear. It had even more mysterious powers than all those. It had powers that stretched men's minds.

One of its powers was that it lengthened the day. Some animals, like the cats in their natural environment, sleep by day and hunt at night. But man belongs to the daytime world. He can work only when he has light, and this the fire gave him. He could work into the night to perfect his tools and weapons. He could sit up and talk, exchange ideas, plan and think and invent. People could talk and think in the dark, but they were more likely to fall asleep. The light of the fire helped them to stay awake.

The Neanderthal men in Europe kept alive through the sixty thousand years of the last era of ice only because of their fire. And it may also have been around the fire that they took the great step of thinking in the way that men think, about such great mysteries as life and death. They were the first creatures on earth to bury their dead, as we know, and to leave them tools and weapons to use in a life after death. No creature of any kind had thought of such things before.

By lengthening the day and the waking hours, firelight naturally shortened the night and the sleeping. The more hours men spent awake, the more they used their minds and the more their minds grew. And there was something else that happened. In every family or band of these early people, there was at least one member who did not sleep at all through the night, or who woke up every so often, all night long, to tend the fire that kept them from freezing or being attacked by lurking beasts.

The fire tender was the guardian of all their lives. It could not be one of the strong young men, the hunters. They tramped many miles, fought and conquered the quarry, and butchered and carried home the kill. They endured danger, weariness and bitter cold all the time they were away from the cave. When they came home, they could only eat and fall into an exhausted sleep. Nor could the young active women stay awake—those who cared for the children, gathered wood for the fire, and brought in supplies of plant foods in case the hunt should fail. The fire could be left only to one of the old ones.

The old one would not be very old in actual years. At a time when human beings rarely lived past the age of thirty, the old one might be between forty and fifty. Until there was fire, any member of the band who was too old to hunt or work was useless, only another mouth to feed, and in hard times an old man or an old woman might not be kept alive. But when fire came into men's lives, the old ones were important.

The old ones could be trusted with the fire. They would be wise and experienced in keeping alive the precious embers. They might also be wise in other things, like the strategies of hunting, the tending of injuries and illnesses, the plants that could be used as medicine. As guardians of the life-preserving magic of the fire, they already had a special magic and mystery about them. Such an old man might be the leader, the planner, the priest of the family. Such an old woman might be the nurse who cared for the sick or wounded and helped the women in childbirth.

So the old ones would be of great value, and the younger men and women would do all they could to care for them, bring them food, even chew it soft for them if they had lost their teeth, like the old Neanderthal man in the cave where the roof fell in so many thousands of years ago.

The old ones were also of value to the future of mankind. They were the sturdy ones who had managed to survive hardship, the intelligent ones who had avoided accident, or else they would not have lived to be old. In their long lives they would have many children, and they would hand on to their children their inborn strength and intelligence. Some of their children would also inherit their ability to work on against weariness, putting off sleep, in order to do something important, whether it was tending the fire or perfecting a tool or figuring out a new invention or a new idea.

So the fire acted as a force of natural selection, which chose for the future the mind that could stay awake and think long thoughts through the night while others slept. And this kind of mind became part of the inheritance of future generations of mankind.

The fire gave man one other precious gift, the gift of home. When there was no fire, there was no pressing reason to return to one spot or another to camp. The nearest shelter might be the best just because it was near. The women and children would not be left behind in a safe place with the fire, but instead they would trudge after the hunters, and run up to squat beside the kill and rend and eat their share like the beasts.

But when there was a fire, someone would be left behind to tend it, and the sick and injured and the very young children could be left in that person's care. The men would come back from their hunting and the women from their food-gathering to its welcome warmth and safety. The men might go a hundred miles on a single hunt, but they tramped the long way back, carrying great haunches of meat to feed the women and children, the old ones and the sick.

Where there was fire there was home and comfort, time to eat and time to tell tales of the day's adventures, with an appreciative audience to listen. The animals had their lairs, but man, at last, had a home.

In Europe there are caves where families of the Stone Age hunters lived year after year for thousands and thousands of years. The cave became the place where tools were chipped and shaped, where animal skins were scraped and cured and stitched into clothing. It was a place where supplies could be stored—good flint for new tools, good hides for new clothes, even some foods that would not quickly spoil.

Later, the depths of some caves became hidden sanctuaries where Stone Age artists painted their magic paintings to draw the game to their spears, and the wise old men danced in costumes of antlers and skins to lure the game with their magic.

By that time, all the early kinds of men had vanished. The man-apes had gone and after them the ape-men, and finally the men who first made their homes in the caves, the Neanderthal men. While the last of the Ice Age glaciers still clung to the land, the Cro-Magnon people alone were left of the primate line that had inherited the seven great gifts.

With them we take up our story again, in the world of thirty-five thousand years ago.

Part 3

The Next 25,000 Years

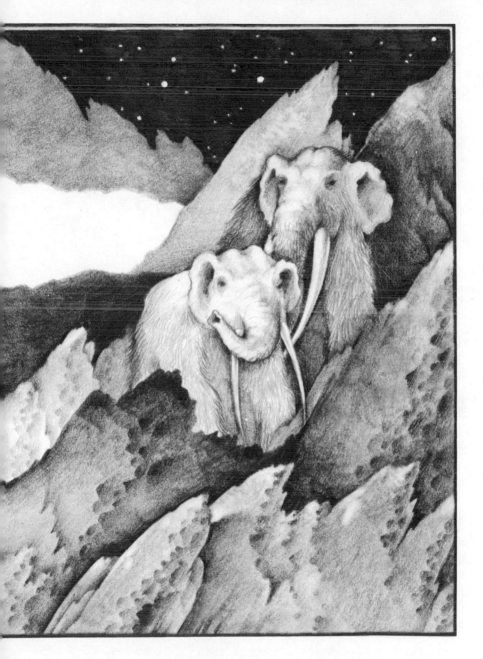

Hunters of the Valley _____

Imagine that a group of us—boys and girls, parents, friends—have set out on a camping trip in a part of the world far from civilization. And imagine that for some reason our equipment—tents, blankets, guns, knives and axes, clothes, cooking gear and even the cans and boxes of food—has all been left behind. Suppose, now, that instead of giving up our trip and turning back, we decide to push on and make the best of things, seeing what we can accomplish by our own efforts.

What kind of camping spot would we look for? First of all we would think of shelter. Then we would want a supply of good fresh water and fuel for our fire. We would want to make sure there were animals nearby that we could hunt for our food. And we would have to have a supply of some material out of which we could make weapons to hunt with, and tools for everything else we would be making for ourselves.

If we were taking our trip thirty-five thousand years ago instead of today, we would find just such a perfect camping and hunting spot in a part of southwestern France called the Dordogne. It was this very spot that our ancestors discovered in Europe during the Ice Age. It is a country threaded with narrow green valleys in which herds of deer and other game would come in those days to browse on the leaves and shoots of shrubs, and drink the cool, clear water of the stream below. The walls of the valleys are cliffs of white limestone, in which the patient dripping of water through long years has hollowed out overhanging eaves and deep natural caves. In the cliffs and strewn on the ground below we would have found quantities of flint, the ideal material for weapons and tools. In these valleys they made their home for thousands of years while the ice came and went just to the north of them.

In the spring the herds moved north through the valley to feed where tender new greenery sprang up at the edges of the melting glacial streams. And in the fall the game passed through again, going south. When the hunting was very good, the families could live in the caves of the Dordogne the year round.

Or the whole tribe would move north for a few weeks in the summer, the women and children and the old ones along with the hunters, and one of the old ones would be carrying the embers of the hearth fire in a hollowed stone. They would make their brief summer camp, no more than a windbreak or lean-to such as we might build for a few nights or a few weeks in the mild season. And when in the early fall the fine weather broke and the storms began to warn of bitter days and nights to come, they would turn back south to the comforting shelter of their caves in the Dordogne.

The game, too, would turn south as the green growth withered during frosty nights and the streams froze over. By November, when the herds of deer, bison, and wild oxen came browsing their way southward, a lookout stationed high up on the cliff above the caves could shout the signal, and the waiting band of hunters could drive the game down the narrow valley. In a few hours they could kill many weeks' supply of meat, skins for clothing, and bone and staghorn for new tools and weapons.

Life was pleasant in the valley through the winter months. The hearth fire at the cave entrance kept out the cold and prowling cave bears, cave lions, wolves, and hyenas as well. The long days between hunts were spent in curing skins, making tools, teaching the boys and girls the skills they needed for this hunting life, spinning tales of other years and other hunts. There was time for carving and decorating a fine weapon, for making strings of animal teeth and beads of bone and horn. There was time for thinking about life and death, spirits and gods.

This was the way of life of the new men who followed the Neanderthal people and lived through the last of the Ice Age in Europe, the next twenty-five thousand years. Their caves are still there, empty and silent above the highway that now runs along the valley floor connecting the French towns and villages of today. In fact it was the workmen, clearing an ancient fall of rock to widen the road in 1868, who first discovered the secret of the caves. And it was some French schoolboys, going to the rescue of their little dog that had fallen into a crevice in the rocks in 1940, who first saw the great animal paintings on walls and ceilings, deep within one of the caves, that had been left by the vanished hunters.

By the time the schoolboys found the cave of Lascaux in France, cave paintings had already been discovered. An-

other dog had led his master into the great painted cave of
Altamira in Spain, at just about the same time the road
builders in France first found the ancient cave dwelling in
the Dordogne.

Until the road builders' discovery, just about a hundred
years ago, few people could imagine that men had lived
on earth so many thousands of years before, or what kind
of men they were. Now the scientists have dug down
through layer after layer of the cave floors, carefully chart-
ing and studying what they find there. All explorers of the
past have to dig, because each year the winds and the rains
and the natural wearing away of rock walls and roofs leave
a layer of debris on the cave floors, and over the thousands
of years the layers become many feet thick.

Digging down through these layers of the past, the explorers find the tools and weapons of the hunters, the
bones of the animals they hunted, and sometimes the remains of the hunters themselves and their wives and children, buried in postures of sleep. The trained eyes of the
scientists read the layers like the pages of a book, from the
top and most recent layer, down, down to the oldest and
farthest back in the long centuries of the Ice Age. In one
such spot above the valley, called Combe Grenal, the explorers have dug down through sixty-four layers and have
read a story that covered eighty-five thousand years.

The Combe Grenal was a campsite of Neanderthal people over those many thousands of years. The Neanderthals
were the first to leave their story in the Dordogne caves,
just as they were the first men we know who faced the bit-

·ter climate of a frozen period in Europe during the Ice Age. They may have been the first men to discover the good caves and the good hunting of the Dordogne valley.

Each layer in the cave floor tells the story of many winters when the families came back, year after year, to live there. We know from many clues that these were their winter homes. One clue is the stacks of antlers that have been found, which show by the state of their growth that the deer were hunted there in the late fall of the year.

In some of the caves a layer of earth without any human trace lies over the Neanderthal layers, and this tells us that the Neanderthal hunters did not return during those winters, that perhaps by then the fierce cold had overcome them. Above that blank page comes the rich story of new men, with new tools, new skills, the endurance and especially the inventiveness to live through the last advances of the ice and the last killing cold of the Ice Age.

These were the Cro-Magnon people, the tall men with high foreheads, broad faces, high-bridged noses, strong chins and large eyes. If they could appear magically today, with their hair cut in a modern barber shop and their beards trimmed or shaved, we might take them for Irishmen or Norwegians or Swedes. They may have been descendants of Neanderthal and other kinds of human beings who mingled in the milder climate of the eastern Mediterranean lands during many thousands of years, and then came into Europe and began to make their homes in the Dordogne caves about thirty-five thousand years ago.

When the Cro-Magnon people came to the Dordogne,

the wild horses and the aurochs, an early kind of ox, were the most plentiful animals to hunt. The huge and deadly cave bear, eight feet of muscle from nose to tail, was still there, and so was the ferocious woolly rhinoceros. There were still the great cave cats, cave lions and cave leopards, and there were hyenas and big northern wolves.

Red deer were all about, and the agile chamois and ibex leaped along the rugged cliffs. Through the centuries that they lived there the ice advanced from the north again and again. Each time the climate turned colder, many of these warm-weather animals disappeared, and the reindeer herds that followed the edges of the ice came south to the Dordogne.

If these people came from a milder land like the shores of Palestine, we may wonder why they stayed to risk the Ice Age cold in Europe. The answer may be that big game was so plentiful. The game had given a plentiful food supply to the Neanderthal people and perhaps the excitement of hunting as well. It now did the same for the new men.

At first the Cro-Magnon people lived and hunted in much the same way as Neanderthal men had done before them. But they had some advantages. They knew how to make fire—a skill which we are not sure the Neanderthals had—and they cooked their food. They also had more efficient tools and more efficient ways of making them.

The earlier toolmakers had simply chipped an edge on a chunk of flint and thrown the chips away, except for those that happened to come off in the shape of good knife blades. The new method was to take a good piece of flint and use it as a core, chipping off pieces of the size and shape that would make a good tool or weapon by itself. With this method a hunter could carry a good piece of flint with him, and whenever he needed it he could chip off a new knife or scraper, a curved blade for a spokeshave to trim a new wooden spear, or a flint spear point to replace the one that was lost or broken in the hunt.

The toolmakers were now quite expert craftsmen. They would prepare a good flint chunk by striking off rough ends so that it had a flat top. Then they rested it on a stone, as a platform or anvil, and struck off pieces of various sizes and shapes as they needed them, all around the core. To do this they did not just hit the core flint with another rock and strike off chips that might or might not come out right. Instead they would use a pointed or wedge-shaped piece of bone or deer horn as a punch, placing it at just the right spot on the edge of the core, and then striking the punch so that the piece would chip off neatly at the thickness that was wanted. This not only saved the labor of cutting a chip to the right size, but it also prevented the waste of flint.

That was one important advance that the Cro-Magnons made in tool manufacture. Another was the invention of the stone chisel. This was a toolmaker's tool, one with which new kinds of tools could be made out of new materials such as deer horn, the ivory of mammoth tusks, or the bone of any big animal.

Flint shatters easily, as we know, and a flint knife blade could not carve these other materials without shattering. The chisel was also made of flint, but it had a narrow edge, sharpened across the grain of the flint, so that it was less likely to shatter. With this narrow and much stronger edge, the toolmaker could carve ivory, horn, and bone almost as easily as he could carve wood.

With this tool the new men made fine, sharp spearheads of horn and bone that would not shatter if the spear happened to strike an animal on the bone. They took to carving hooked barbs along the side of a spear point, and thus invented the harpoon for hunting seals and even whales off the frozen Ice Age shores. They made sharply pointed awls of bone to pierce holes in animal skins and to lace the skins together with thongs for clothing, a more secure way of keeping covered against the cold than just tying the skins on. And from the awl, some brilliant toolmaker developed that most remarkable invention, the needle.

It may have been the women who first thought of the needle. With a needle, a woman could stitch together a fitted coat with sleeves and trousers with legs that would really stay on and keep a man warm while he lay in wait for the game to come within range of his spear. She could make a hood for a child's head, perhaps even fur mittens for his hands. So the toolmakers began to make needles out of bone with their flint chisels. They would cut parallel grooves in the bone to carve out a thin sliver, and then they would carve one end of the sliver to a sharp point and pierce a hole in the other end for the needle's eye. Like all the great inventions of the past it was really very simple— once someone had the idea for it.

With fire and fitted clothing to keep them warm, and with efficient weapons for almost every kind of game—

especially the biggest kinds—the new men spread eastward to the icy steppes of Russia. And they went still farther east, crossing the vast continent of Asia until they reached the shore of the Pacific. There came a time when the great ice sheet melted, but the sea had not yet risen high enough to cover the land bridge between Siberia and Alaska, where now the waters flow in the Bering Strait. That was the time when those great hunters, following the big game across from Asia, traveled southward into the New World.

It may have happened between twenty-eight thousand and twenty-six thousand years ago, when the ice melted for the next-to-last time and then froze over again, trapping both the hunters and the game in the Western Hemisphere. Or it may have been about eleven thousand years ago, when the ice melted for the last time and the land bridge lay high and dry for a while. Until their traces are found, we will not know just when they came. But what is fairly certain is that these new men, the big game hunters of Europe and Asia, became the first Americans.

Hunters of the Plains _____

Other kinds of men besides the Cro-Magnon lived in Europe during those last twenty-five thousand years of the Ice Age. Some were tall, some short and stocky, some small and slender. But they were all hunters. They all lived by hunting the great beasts and they all did their best to survive in the same harsh and icy world.

Although some of these different peoples may have come

in small bands from nearby Asian lands or across the land bridges from Africa and stayed only a brief time, some found ways to stay longer, perhaps five thousand years at a stretch. To us that is a long time, when we consider that the history of our own Western world, from the ancient Greeks until today, is only about half as long—a little more than twenty-five hundred years. But time still moved slowly, and in the last twenty-five thousand years of the Ice Age there was still little change in the way men lived their lives.

In western Europe, as we know, men lived mostly in caves. But they also lived where there were no caves, and with the human talent for invention they found a different way to survive through the icy times. These people were the mammoth hunters of the plains.

Europe at the time was cut almost into two continents by the impassable ice. The Arctic glacier reached down from the north, and stretching almost to meet it was the great Alpine glacier in the very center of Europe. It spread out like a vast, glittering skirt far beyond the feet of the mountains, almost completely cutting off the western from the eastern continent.

To the east lay the steppes, the broad prairies that still form the heart of eastern Europe from Russia southward to the Carpathian Mountains. On these plains the grasses grew tall in the warm season, and great herds of mammoths came to graze, moving north in the spring and south again in the fall along regular grazing routes.

Mammoths roamed in western Europe as well, and the

western people hunted them. They painted pictures of mammoths on their cave walls in France, and one picture shows a mammoth caught in a trap or pitfall. But for the Ice Age men in eastern Europe the mammoth was the most important game animal. It was their very special source of meat, skins, bone, tusk ivory, clothing, building material, and nearly everything else they needed in order to live.

We know exactly how the mammoths looked, not only from their fossil bones and the cave paintings of them, but because some years ago a number of them were found by explorers in Siberia. The animals were frozen whole, just as they had perished so many thousands of years ago in the ice. Mammoths were a great-grandfather species of elephant, with trunks, tusks, and skimpy tails like the elephants we know, except that instead of wrinkled gray hide they had coats of shaggy reddish hair that kept them warm. But their tusks were murderously long and curved, and the beasts themselves were huge—even compared to modern elephants—with high, humped shoulders and a long, sloping back. Some of them stood nine feet and some as much as thirteen and one-half feet tall at the shoulder. A whole tribe of hunters and their wives and children could live well for many weeks on the meat of one mammoth.

Men had to be both courageous and intelligent to hunt such formidable beasts, and these men were both. We do not know exactly how they hunted, for they left no large weapons with which such animals could have been killed. We must guess that they took advantage of the shape of the land, and that bands of men shouting and waving torches drove the herds over cliffs, as the Neanderthal men had done long before, or drove them into ravines in which they could be killed by boulders dropped on them from above. From the masses of mammoth bones that they left, we know that in the several thousand years during which these men lived and hunted on the plains, they killed and feasted on hundreds of thousands of the great animals.

Where the mammoth hunters showed their originality was in their living arrangements. This was no hospitable land like the Dordogne Valley in southern France. The plains were swept by fierce winds, often carrying blinding clouds of yellow dust, called loess, which the glaciers deposited at their edges as they melted, froze, and melted again, year after year. Today the loess is a most fertile topsoil, lying many feet deep over eastern Europe. It was spread there during the Ice Age, in what must have been the wildest kind of dust storms. Blizzards, too, howled across the plains, piling snow to great depths. In such a climate, anything smaller than a mammoth could not survive without shelter. There were no cliffs honeycombed with convenient caves, so the mammoth hunters made their own. They were the first known house builders.

They did not build on top of the windswept land—they dug into it. They dug pit houses in the ground, set boulders into the earth walls to keep them from crumbling, and pounded rock dust on the bottom for a floor that would let moisture drain through and not become a sea of mud. To roof the house over, they spread mammoth hides which they fastened down around the edges with heavy mammoth bones.

Some of the pit houses were quite large, with space for more than one family to live. Some were round with the skin roof raised and domed, probably on some sort of brushwood framework, for there were few trees growing on the plains to provide posts. One such round house in Czechoslovakia was partly dug into a hillside, and it had an outer wall made of limestone and clay. This was the first time, so far as we know, that men had built a wall.

The mammoth hunters built their hearth fires year after year in the same places, and they show a record of thousands of years of human living. On the plains there was no wood for fires, but the hunters had discovered long ago that dried bones would burn. These men also discovered another fuel, a black shiny rock that was actually not rock, but coal. Coal lies close to the surface of the ground in some of the eastern countries, and in the days of the mammoth hunters the winds and the moving glaciers must have laid it bare. Some observant hunter—perhaps one of the old men or old women who guarded the fire—must one day have piled some of these black rocks as a windbreak to keep the precious embers from being blown away. And in that way, perhaps, the people made the enormous discovery that this peculiar kind of shiny black rock would burn.

The mammoth hunters chose their house sites with care in order to find the best shelter from the winds and also to be near the routes that the mammoth herds followed every year to and from their grazing grounds. Near the houses the people stored their mammoth bones in orderly piles like a farmer's well-stacked woodpile. The bones of different lengths and shapes were piled separately, the wide hip bones in one stack, the long leg bones in another, the skulls in a third. These were valuable stores out of which came the fuel for fires, the anchors that held down a roof, the raw material for tools and weapons.

This precious material served still another purpose. Mammoth bones were used as a ceremonial wall around the mammoth hunters' burial places. These people, too, buried their dead with reverence and care.

One such graveyard, found at a place called Predmost in Czechoslovakia, was walled all around with neatly laid mammoth shoulder blades and skulls. Within the wall, closely placed in a squatting position, were the bodies of about fifty people of all ages. One was a child with a necklace of ivory beads still around its neck. Over the top of the cemetery was a layer of stones sixteen inches thick, a protection for the bodies from prowling wolves and hyenas. To the people of that time, perhaps it was also a protection for the living against the wandering souls of the dead.

The mammoth hunters were skilled toolmakers who made good flint choppers and knives to cut up the huge beasts for food. They sharpened their knives as we do, on only one edge, leaving the other edge smooth and rounded so that a man could press his fingers against it without cutting himself when he was doing fine work on bone or ivory. They made bracelets, pins and necklaces of pierced shells, animal teeth, and ivory from mammoth tusks. They had chisels and they also had a tool they themselves had developed, a fine small blade of flint, suitable for carving and engraving. It is called a gravette, and from it the mammoth hunters have been given the name of Gravettians. It was a tool they used in creating their own particular form of art—for it was in this time that art was born.

With inventiveness and intelligence equal to our own, the men of these last twenty-five thousand years of the Ice Age had something that the Neanderthal and other men before them never had—the leisure to make objects of art and decoration.

The hunters of the valley, living in their caves, developed one kind of art, and the hunters of the plain in their pit houses developed another. Fortunately they left us many examples of both kinds, telling us a great deal about the minds and imaginations of these mighty hunters of long ago.

The First Artists

Deep within the caves of southwestern France and nearby Spain are the world's oldest art galleries. Great black bulls, larger than life, are drawn leaping across the ceiling of one of these caves. Bison, wild oxen, woolly rhinoceroses, hairy mammoths, lions and lionesses stand and run along the walls of other caves. Sometimes the figures are sculptured, where the artist cleverly used a rounded part of the rock wall to show an animal's shoulder or rump or a long projection of stone that suggested a leg.

Sometimes the artist hacked out the shape of the animal with his flint chisel, and sometimes he spread a layer of damp clay on the cave wall and engraved the outline of his picture before he painted it. In the center of one cave chamber, crouched on the floor, are two clay sculptures, one of a cave lion and the other of a cave bear.

Some of the animals are shown trapped or already slain. Some have their hearts outlined or painted in red, and some have other vital points on their bodies circled where a spear thrust would be most effective. Some of the female animals are shown pregnant. The animals are marvelously lifelike and alive. Those hunters knew every line and motion of the beasts they hunted, and that does not surprise us. What is astonishing is that men of so long ago, living a life so difficult and dangerous, were able to develop such artistic skill.

Some of the paintings are in black, or black and red, and some are in many colors. Here and there a human hand is painted—just a hand. Sometimes there are figures of men among the animals, but they are not usually hunters. They are men strangely dressed, in animal skins and with horns, paws, a tail, and an animal mask, and they seem to be dancing. In some of the cave art chambers there are footprints in the earth floor, as though men had danced there.

The paintings were done during the last fifteen thou-

sand years of the Ice Age, from twenty-five thousand to
about ten thousand years ago. We know a great deal about
how the paintings were done, for the artists left some of
their tools and materials behind in the caves where modern explorers have found them.

We know that they made their paints out of earths that
were naturally colored by metallic ores. Ocherous earth,
containing iron oxide, gave them red, yellow, and orange
colors, and earth containing manganese oxide gave them
shades of brown and a bluish black. For true black they
used the carbon of burned animal bones. They pounded
these earths in hollow stones and mixed them with animal
fat to blend them and animal blood to make them dry
hard on the wall.

We have some of the stone mortars and pestles they used
to grind and mix their paints. We have some of the containers in which they stored the prepared paints—shells,
hollowed stones, and the long leg bones of animals which
they filled like tubes and fitted with stoppers. There are
still traces of paint in them, telling us what they were used
for.

The artists used flat stones or bones as palettes, and
they put the paint on the wall with their fingers, or with
some sort of brush such as they could have made out of a
twig with its end chewed or pounded, or with a pad of
moss or animal fur. For their most delicate work they took
a mouthful of paint and blew it through a long bone, an
early version of today's spray-painting. Experts who have
examined the work have told us all this about the cave
artists' techniques.

The artists also left us some of their sketchbooks, flat pieces of stone or bone on which they sketched out their work either for practice or when they were planning a full-size painting on the cave wall. They left us their lamps, hollowed stones in which animal fat burned with a floating wick of animal or plant fiber. By the uncertain light of such lamps they painted their stunning paintings in those deep, dark cave chambers in the heart of the cliff far from the daylight.

But even though we know all this, the cave paintings are still full of mystery. Why did they choose to paint in such hidden chambers, as though their paintings were secret for some reason and not supposed to be seen? Some of the art chambers are so deep that to reach them the artists themselves had to crawl as much as three-quarters of a mile along passages so cramped that in places a man has to squirm through on his belly.

Why, in some places, did they paint so high on ceilings and walls that they must have had to sit on the shoulders of other men to do the work?

Why did they mark the heart and other vital spots where an animal could suffer a mortal wound? Why did they paint the human figures wearing their strange animal disguises, and why were they dancing?

Like good detectives, we have to find one solution to the mystery that will answer all these questions. And there is a

Deep inside the home cave, an Ice Age artist paints pictures of the animals his people hunt. His work is illuminated by a lamp made with a wick burning in animal fat in a hollowed-out stone.

solution. But to arrive at it, we have to do again what we did when we first set out on this adventure. We have to wipe our minds clear of history and especially of science, and try to put ourselves into the minds of those ancient hunters. We have to try to see the world brand-new, as they did, and find explanations as they did for the events that they did not understand.

It is a gift of our human intelligence to be curious, to try to understand the how and why of things. Those men of twenty-five thousand years ago had the same human intelligence that we have, and they used it in the same way that we do. What they did not have were our scientific tools and our historical record of scientific research and experiment. They had only the knowledge they gained by their own keen senses, the memory of what they had seen and experienced, and their human reasoning power to put their observations together and find meaning in it all.

They experienced winds, storms, cold, the change of seasons, the freezing and melting of the ice. They saw the sky clear or covered with clouds, the sun shining warm by day and the cold bright stars at night and a moon that grew big and small and sometimes vanished entirely. They saw the sky sometimes lit by blinding streaks and flashes and heard it roar like no earthly animal.

They saw the herds of game on which their life depended, coming and going along the same paths at the same time each season. Sometimes the game was plentiful and sometimes it was scarce. Sometimes the hunt was successful and sometimes not. They wondered what lay behind all this.

They knew fire, a great wonder. They knew that a fire lived and died. When it died, what went out of it? They knew that men lived and died. When a man died, what went out of him? They knew that a man could lie sleeping in the cave, and yet at the same time he could be going on a hunt, fighting a beast, suffering a wound, feeling excitement, hope, fear, pain. And he would wake up again in the same place where he lay down, with no spear in his hand, no wound on his body, not even tired from his mysterious hunt but actually rested and ready for the real hunt of the day. When this happened, what went out of him to hunt while his body lay sleeping in the cave?

His answer was—for him—logical. What went out hunting while he slept, what left a man's body when the man died was an unseen self, a spirit self. Everything around him must also have a spirit self—wind, ice, storm, water gushing from a spring, sun, moon, stars. Only a spirit self could explain them all and the ways they behaved. The beasts must have a spirit which guided them on their way and left them when they died. The man had made his spear himself but it, too, must have a spirit, otherwise why did it sometimes willfully swerve from the course and miss the beast?

The fire most surely had a great and dangerous spirit which could hurt him and even kill him if he was careless. The bravest of the beasts knew this and were afraid of the fire. Yet he, man, had found a way to tame and control the fire, feed it and protect it and make it serve him.

If he could tame the spirit of the fire, surely he could tame the other spirits, or at least gain some control over them. In the same way that the spirit hunter in his dream was a picture of himself, the spirit of the animal might be captured in a picture of the animal, and it could be killed by the pictured spirit of his spear. Then in the real hunt the same success could be really achieved, just as in the real hunt the same kinds of things happened as he had experienced in his dreams.

Human beings enjoyed painting, carving, decorating the things of everyday life and making ornaments for themselves. As soon as they became efficient enough at the serious business of staying alive—getting food and shelter, keeping warm, keeping safe from dangerous beasts— people began to make pretty things. They carved beads of bone and ivory to hang around the neck of a wife or child. They made their flint tools in forms that were beautiful and graceful as well as practical, and they decorated objects of bone and horn with carvings. And so they could have painted their splendid animal pictures just for enjoyment. But if pleasure was their purpose, they would hardly have placed their paintings so far from the daylight and the warm fire, where it would not have been pleasant to paint them.

Perhaps the beads and the carvings on tools and weapons had a purpose besides simple enjoyment. We just do not know. But the cave paintings surely did. They had the serious purpose of capturing the spirit of the game and controlling it and so bringing success with the living beasts in the hunt.

After all it is not such a strange idea. Even we in our modern scientific world sometimes feel much the same about a photograph of someone we love. Sentimental lovers of old times used to kiss the picture and feel in some way that they were kissing the person. Nowadays we are more likely just to keep it in sight and look at it, and enjoy the feeling that the loved person is present at least in our thoughts. Scientists who go to study primitive people today still have some trouble taking photographs, because when the people see themselves pictured they are afraid that some harm might be done to them through the picture if it were to fall into the hands of an unfriendly person.

Some tribes in Australia, Asia, and the Amazon jungle, who still live in a way not very different from the cave men, have a very elaborate way of dealing with the unseen spirits of everything around them—wind, rain, rocks, trees, animals, people. Some very advanced American Indian tribes had marvelous ways of curing the sick by spirit methods, and they were often successful, because the sick people believed in them and getting well often depends a little upon the sick person's confidence in his cure.

We call these spirit methods magic, meaning that they are based on beliefs and not on scientific laws and observed and proven facts. But we can be respectful of this magic of long ago, because it was the science of the men of long ago. It was their intelligent explanation of what they observed in nature, the best they could do without tools and without experiment, and they used it intelligently within those limits to gain control of nature for their welfare and the improvement of their lives.

The hunters built up an elaborate system for their hunting magic through those many centuries in the caves. The painters were such skilled artists that they must have been excused, at least part of the time, from hunting and other tasks just to paint, and to teach their art to their sons and other young men who were to become artists.

And the dancing man in the animal mask and horns, wearing an animal skin with paws and a tail, was also a specialist. He was the leader of the magic, the priest of the tribe. We would call him a medicine man or a witch doctor. He led the ceremonies, and he was the one who knew the right words and the right dances that would gain power over the spirits. His special knowledge, too, would be handed down to a chosen successor. The mask and the disguise may have begun as a real hunting technique, a way of creeping up on the animals, as the American Indians of the plains used to disguise themselves in a bison skin and horns to hunt the bison in the days before they had horses. In the magic ceremony the disguise would have taken on magic power, giving the dancing priest control over the spirits of the animals.

The pictures sometimes show a spear flying toward the animal or a track through the animal's body that the spear should take. The hunting dance imitated the hunt even more closely. In the chamber of the lion and the bear, the clay sculpture of the bear still has visible marks where spears were thrust into it. Probably the sculptured animals were dressed in actual animal skins, complete with head and paws, for a bear's skull was found still lying between the clay animal's paws.

The hunters wanted not only success in the hunt but plentiful game for hunting, and so the pictures show pregnant female animals, to make the herds increase and multiply. They also wanted their own families and clans to increase and multiply, so that there would be no lack of strong men for the hunting. And so they made images of pregnant women.

These images were not cave paintings but statues a few inches high. And they were invented not by the cave artists but by the mammoth hunters of the eastern plains. These were their special contribution to Ice Age art, these little statues carved out of limestone or soapstone or the ivory of mammoth tusks, or made of earth clay and baked in the hearth fire or more likely in a special kiln by the clan priest or medicine man.

The figures are shown without any clothing, except sometimes a girdle or fringed belt and sometimes a cap on the head or a crown of the woman's own braided hair. They are strange little statues because they show no facial features and sometimes no face, and often there is only a knob for the head and little rounded ends for the feet. All the artist's care was in shaping and emphasizing the breasts and belly and hips of the female, the parts of the body having to do with childbearing, because those were the parts on which they wanted to exercise their magic so that the women would be fertile.

We can imagine that these people wondered a great deal about the mystery of birth and new life and tried to help the birth of a baby with the strongest possible magic.

Primitive peoples living in our own time still do. There is an old belief that to lead an animal across the body of a woman laboring in childbirth would give the woman some of the animal's strength. We know just how ancient that belief is, because a carving on reindeer bone, found in one of the Ice Age caves, shows part of just such a ceremony, a reindeer stepping across the body of a pregnant woman lying on her pallet on the cave floor.

The art of making the mysterious statues of pregnant women spread westward along the shores of the Mediterranean into Italy and France, and the making of statues and other magic for fertility went on for thousands of years, long after the Ice Age hunters who first made them had vanished. Fertility magic became more and more important in the great revolution that changed men's way of life from hunting to farming, from killing animals in the wild to taming and domesticating them. Then fertility became crucial, and more important even than the fertility of animals and human beings was the fertility of the earth.

The great change was coming. But there were other changes that had to come first.

A Time of Change _____

Through the last five thousand years of the Ice Age the hunting peoples rose to their highest achievements in art and skills. Their cave paintings became dazzling in their many colors and the aliveness of their animals, and they had become such successful hunters that they had time to turn almost every article of their daily lives into a work of art. They decorated even their harpoon heads (for us this would be like carving beautiful designs not only on our hunting rifles but on the bullets to be fired from them).

They made all kinds of ornaments to wear—bracelets, anklets, pins and brooches, necklaces of many strands with spacers to keep the strands separated. They made their jewelry of every kind of material—stone, bone, antler horn, tusk ivory, amber, shells, and the vertebrae from fish spines. These materials from the sea have been found so far inland that there must have been a good deal of trading going on across great distances, even in Ice Age Europe.

With their good bone needles, the women were making stitched and fitted clothing out of animal hides, and the fine eyes of the needles tell us that they were able to work with quite thin strips of hide or perhaps animal tendons for their thread. They still buried their dead sprinkled with the lifelike red of ocherous earth, and they laid them to rest fully dressed in their clothes of skin and fur. When the graves were opened in our own time, the necklaces were still draped around the necks, the bracelets and anklets still adorned the ancient bones, and all around the reverently buried dead were the beautiful decorated tools, weapons, and personal ornaments that they had treasured in life.

Since the tall Cro-Magnon people, many different strains of people had been living the hunting life in Europe, and these last and greatest artists of the Ice Age were the

Magdalenians. Their name, like so many of the others including the Cro-Magnon, is taken from the French village near the cave where their remains were first found. They were a small, gracefully built people with delicate bones, a gifted people who filled the rugged life of the hunter in an icy world with things of great beauty and elegance. Their most valuable game animal was the reindeer, an animal of the Arctic, and their cave homes in the Dordogne were still at the edge of an arctic world.

But now the world was changing. Year by year the average temperature was warming, only a fraction of a degree at a time but enough to begin the melting of the great ice sheets. As the Alpine glacier melted, it released streams of water which became torrents rushing down the mountainsides, deepening old valleys and cutting new ones. As the Arctic glacier retreated northward, it gouged out hollows in the land, piled up ridges of soil, gravel, and boulders that it had dragged along in its icy grip for many miles and then dropped as it melted. Often the glacier left a dam of scrambled rocks and soil across a valley, and the valley filled with water to form a bog, a vast marsh, or a deep lake.

At first the change was slow, but presently it became faster and faster. Like a monster plow, the receding glacier churned up the land. Soon, well-watered and basking in sunshine, the earth began to put forth green life. The seasons came and went as always, but for the earth, freed from its icy prison, it was like a thousand-year springtime.

The last swift transformation came between eleven

thousand and ten thousand years ago. The mantle of sparse tundra grasses turned to flowering meadows. Then shrubby copses sprang up, and woodlands of water-loving alder and willow. Hillsides became covered with dark evergreens and slender birches. In the bogs and marshes, thick swamp forests grew, and over the dry places spread forests of oak, elm, linden, and all the familiar leafy trees of our temperate zone. All across Europe, the forest stood so thick and unbroken that a squirrel could travel from the Baltic to the Atlantic shore in the treetops without once having to set foot on the ground.

As the forests grew, the big game dwindled. The great grazing animals could not live except on grassy plains, and so the hairy mammoth and woolly rhinoceros died out, and with them the fierce cave animals that had lived on them. The reindeer followed the arctic tundra northward, and red deer now roamed the newly grown woodlands.

For the Ice Age hunters it was the end of the world. The Magdalenians, especially, had made their living out of the reindeer herds which supplied them with meat, clothing, and the raw material for weapons and tools. Some of the hunters and their families followed the herds north and never returned to their caves. The remains of a camp of these reindeer hunters, still clinging to their Ice Age ways, have been uncovered in northern Germany near Hamburg, where in the late Ice Age there had been a lake.

But they could not stay there either, for the forests still grew steadily toward them from the south, the ice still retreated northward, and the reindeer followed the ice.

Where these determined reindeer hunters followed their game into the Arctic Circle, how long they survived there, and whether their descendants are among the peoples who now live in the far north—the Laplanders who still follow the reindeer or the Eskimos who compete with the polar bears in hunting the seals—are questions to which we may some day find the answers.

For a while, those who stayed behind hunted the red deer as they had hunted the reindeer. For a thousand years or so, still making their homes in caves, they hunted in the forests. But they never became woodsmen or carpenters and their toolmaking was mainly of small flint points, which they set in a row on a handle like sawteeth for cutting or chopping. Their art consisted of strangely painted pebbles suggesting human figures, which may have been good-luck charms or magic talismans.

Across the Pyrenees in southeastern Spain lived another kind of people, roving hunters who may have gone back and forth across the land bridge between Europe and North Africa. They seem not to have cared about settling down in permanent dwellings, but they left a record of themselves in rock paintings, out in the open and not in caves, that is very gay and lively. They drew hunters leaping, running, pursuing the game, women in elaborate dress standing in groups as though at a ceremony. One painting shows a man or woman clinging to a cliff, gathering honey in a skin bag, while all around the angry bees are buzzing. Others show groups of men charging and fighting each other.

The men in these pictures are hardly more than stick figures, such as a child might draw, but they are wonderfully animated and full of movement. And there is one more surprise in these rock pictures, something we have not seen before. These men are hunting and fighting with bows and arrows.

This new invention came into Europe in the late Ice Age, probably from Africa. The arrow would be too light for the really big game of earlier times, the mammoth and rhinoceros, but it was a fine weapon against swift-moving deer and small game. The bowstring by itself was a splendid new tool, one that would greatly speed up the slow task of starting a fire and would provide an automated drill for the new woodworking crafts that were now beginning. (To use a bowstring as a fire-starter or a drill, wind the string around a pointed stick, set the stick, point down, in the shavings to be lighted or the spot to be drilled, and pull. The bowstring keeps the stick whirling faster than hands can.)

Meanwhile, life was not good in the forest. Where tall trees grew close together there was little sun on the forest floor, and little underbrush grew there for the game to feed on. And so the more energetic people left the caves at last and began to settle in the open places.

Around lakes and marshes the deer, elk, wild ox, and wild pig browsed at the forest edge, small game scampered, and there were birds, water fowl, and fish. When the ice withdrew, it left the Baltic Sea a vast lake and the North Sea mostly dry land. Deep lakes lay in the high valleys and

meadowlands of the Alps, and lakes, marshes, and swamp-
land dotted northern Europe from Russia to England.

The people became lake dwellers and bog dwellers, and
some went to live on islands and seashores. They became
hunter-fisher folk, and gatherers of nuts, berries, edible
plants and roots in the lush green land that was now their
world. They learned to make rafts and boats out of marsh
reeds tied together, and dugout canoes out of hollowed
logs, and they cut poles and paddles of wood to propel
them. They built houses out of reeds and set them on platforms on log stilts over the water, or they built huts of
logs and reed thatch on the shore.

They made snares out of grasses for small game and
waterfowl. They went fishing in their boats with nets of
grass fibers, with fish spears that had bone points or tips
shaped like a pair of toothed jaws, or with fishing lines and
bone fishhooks. The seashore dwellers gathered shellfish
on the shore and fish from the sea. They hunted seals with
clubs, and made boats of sealskin in which they went after
whales and big fish with barbed bone harpoons to which a
line was fastened so that they could pull in the fish when it
was caught.

As the forests grew, the people discovered that here at
hand was a wonderful new material, wood. They could
chop down a tree with the Old Stone Age hand ax, but
somewhere along the way they discovered a great improvement, an ax with a handle. One of the first of these was
made whole out of a deer antler, with one sharpened
prong to form the cutting edge. But these men had long

known how to fit a stone or bone spear point to a wooden
spear, and they soon fitted a stone ax blade to a wooden
handle. The adze, for scraping and hollowing logs, came
next, and gouges, drills, and a whole kit of carpenter's
tools. They made wooden boats and ranged up and down
the coasts. They invented the sledge and dragged their
game home over land and winter snow instead of carrying
it on their backs.

Some of the peoples of this time in Europe ate human
flesh, and some made human sacrifices. Cannibalism has
come down from very ancient times, and with most of the
peoples who have practiced it, the eating of some part of a
human being has been ceremonial and religious rather
than simply for food. Warriors would eat the heart of a
brave enemy they had killed to gain some of his courage.
When a chief or a respected elder died, his people would
eat small portions of the body to gain his wisdom or to per-
petuate his greatness in their own bodies, a mark of highest respect. The earliest ape-men, who left human remains
in their caves in China, may have been cannibals out of
hunger. But since that time, very few human societies have
eaten human flesh except as a solemn ceremony.

The cave-men hunters of the Ice Age left some traces of
these practices in their caves. They buried with dead with
reverence, but they also kept human skulls in a special
place in the cave, as though in a shrine. They placed skulls
of the cave bear in the same way, as though to placate this
fierce enemy or to gain control over his kind. Later in
human history some peoples have used human skulls as

drinking cups that had special magic properties. And there have of course been head hunters, who kept the skulls as trophies of their prowess in war.

The hunter-fisher people of the lakes and bogs continued some of these practices. Burial pits have been found containing human skulls sprinkled with red ocher and all carefully placed to face the setting sun. In one such pit in Bavaria there were twenty-seven skulls, four of men and the rest of women and children, and all had died by violence. Campsites along the Baltic shore have been discovered where human as well as animal bones were among the remains. We can only guess whether they were victims killed for food, sacrificial victims, slain enemies, or members of the tribe who died and were ceremonially eaten.

The people of this time in northern Europe are called the Maglemosians, from a Danish word meaning "great bog." The time is called the Middle Stone Age, because it was different from the Old Stone Age of the big game hunters and not yet the New Stone Age of farming and domestic animals. But these people did have one domestic animal, the dog.

It is a question whether men tamed the dog or the dog adopted men. Wild wolf packs raided the camps of the Old Stone Age hunters for whatever scraps they could pick up after the hunt, and the hunters drove them off and sometimes hunted them. But true dogs appeared in this Middle Stone Age, smaller than the northern wolves and different in other ways in their bony structure and anatomy, and they may have come wandering up from the south as the weather warmed.

For hunting in the forests of this green world, a dog's keen nose could be a great aid. If a dog came sniffing around the camp, he might be thrown a scrap or a bone and he might be tolerated as a scavenger, perhaps also as a watchdog to warn the sleeping men of raiding animals or human enemies. But if once he went along on the hunt and showed himself a good tracker and retriever, then he would become a member of the community, one that earned his keep. Men may have begun by making pets of dogs and ended by recognizing them as good hunting companions. So the dog became a friend of man in this Middle Stone Age in Europe.

Far to the south of the forest lands a very different way of life had already begun in which a tame dog was nothing special, where men already had tame cattle, goats, donkeys, camels, and had begun to tame the earth itself. In the southern lands across the Mediterranean, the end of the Ice Age had come as a disaster, and men had had to find a dramatically new way of life. There a historic revolution began.

Part 4

The Great Revolution

When the Green Lands Withered _____

All through the Ice Age, while the glacier lay over most of Europe, the Mediterranean shores of the two neighboring continents of Africa and Asia had been a rich feeding ground for game of all kinds. Grasses waved thick on the coastal plains, and shrubs and woodlands covered the hillsides. The wild creatures lived well, and so did the men who hunted them for food.

Now, as the ice melted away and the northern lands became well watered, warm, and green, these lands to the south withered and died. The grass turned brown and sere and finally ceased to grow, and over the years the green plains of northern Africa and western Asia became the deserts that they are today, vast seas of blowing sand. Men, beasts, birds, insects, and all growing things huddled together on oases, green islands in the desert where water flowed in springs out of the earth. Life clustered, too, in the narrow valley and on the spreading delta of the Nile, the one great river that still ran across northern Africa to the sea.

On the eastern shore of the Mediterranean the change was more gentle. Streams still flowed out of the hills, some rains still fell, and the land continued friendly to animals and men. Cave-dwelling hunters had lived and thrived here through all the thousands of years while their brothers struggled to survive in ice-locked Europe. The first Neanderthal men and the first Cro-Magnon men had made their way into Europe from here. Here is where the great revo lution now began, in the eastern curve of the Mediterranean that is now Palestine, Syria, and Iraq, and in Anatolia, the Asian part of Turkey. The same revolution came much later in the New World, and according to some very recent discoveries in Thailand, it may have come as much as five thousand years earlier in Southeast Asia.

The women and children of the hunting people showed the way to this revolution. Through the hunting years, while the men went out in their bands to track the big game, the women and children had been gathering other food close to home. Nuts, berries, wild fruits of all kinds, leaves and roots, honey from the wild bees' hives, succulent caterpillars and locusts—all these were good to eat. We can imagine the agile boys and girls clambering up the trees like monkeys and robbing birds' nests of their eggs and fledgling birds, as indeed the monkeys do.

When the game was scarce and the hunting poor, these foods were very welcome. And in times of real famine, such food as the women and children could find might save the families from starving. Even a dinner of dry roots was better than no dinner at all.

Some kinds of food would keep and could be stored. Seeds were such a food. Year after year the women found the same grasses growing in the same spots near their cave homes, grasses that bore good plump seeds when they were ripe. Somewhere along the way the women noticed also that where they had dumped the seeds they did not need, the grasses grew the following season. Little by little they took to scattering their extra supply of seeds on purpose, so that they could gather the crop of grain the next year.

Taming the animals began in much the same way, half by accident, half by plan. The first animal that came to live with men here, as in the north, was the dog, and it came more or less of its own free will and became an equal partner in the hunt. But the next animals to come were of a different kind. They were the sheep and goats and wild cattle that traveled together in herds and ate leaves and grass.

In the old days these animals had been hunted along with the bigger game, the mammoth and rhinoceros. Often it happened that the hunters would bring home a lamb or kid or young calf, and the family would make a pet of it. Sometimes its mother came along, and they might take her milk for their own use if she would not be too skittish to stand still and be milked. But keeping a pet goat or sheep was not the same as keeping a flock or a herd, any more than planting an occasional crop of grass seeds was farming.

To change men's whole way of life some other change had to occur, one that would seriously interfere with the old way. As long as the hunting was good, there was no reason to change. But when the forests spread in the north and the grassy plains turned to deserts in the south, the big game vanished from both places. The food-gathering of the women and children became more and more important. Families came to depend on their crops of grain seeds. And the idea was also born that if a herd could be rounded up for killing, it could be rounded up for capture as well, and the animals could be kept alive and slaughtered as the meat was needed. Better still, they could be bred in captivity, and the herds would grow without animals having to be captured over and over.

This change could take place only where the right kinds of grasses grew and the right kinds of animals roamed. It could not happen in the forest lands of Europe, or on the desert lands of northern Africa. Indeed in some parts of the world, men never did make this revolutionary leap from hunting to farming. Those were parts of the world where grains did not happen to grow wild and herd animals that could be tamed did not happen to live. Australia was such a place, and the Australian natives were still living as Old Stone Age hunters when the Europeans came. The Europeans brought grain and garden seeds, orchard trees, and sheep.

Wool and mutton are Australia's main export products today. But the Australian aborigines could never have become farmers and sheepherders by themselves, not because they lacked the intelligence—for in fact they are the world's most remarkable hunters and trackers—but because on their entire continent there were no native plants or animals that could be tamed for their use.

On the eastern shore of the Mediterranean, and farther inland on the hills above the Arabian and Persian deserts, there were both the plants and the animals to be tamed. Wild goats browsed on the hillsides, and farther north were wild sheep. On the meadows grew the kinds of grasses that we call grains or cereals, which had heads of thick nourishing seeds when they ripened.

These lands, curving like a crescent around the eastern end of the Mediterranean Sea, were the birthplace of the new way of life. Here grew the wild wheat, millet, and barley that the hunting families first used to gather wild and then, when the hunting began to fail, they learned to plant. Here also browsed the wild goats that at first they hunted to kill and then learned to capture and keep as tame herds. Toward the Caspian Sea in the north the more plentiful animals were sheep, and there the first flocks were of sheep rather than goats.

The farmers who domesticated the goats gained milk, meat, and goatskins which they made into bottles and containers as well as clothing. The farmers who tamed the sheep gained all these new products, besides quantities of fat for cooking, for sheep are fatter than goats. And both of them gained another valuable product, wool. We think of wool as coming only from sheep, but the finest wools, angora and cashmere, come from goats. They are quite special breeds of goats, whose ancestors roamed wild in Asia, and their names tell us where they came from. Angora is the same as Ankara, the capital of Turkey, and cashmere is the English spelling of Kashmir, a beautiful mountain district of India. Goat's wool is also called mohair.

While the big game still lived in this part of the world and the weather was cold, the people had furs to wear. For a long time they used the whole pelt of the goats and sheep that they killed for food. The women may have begun to spin and weave with vegetable fibers, such as the wild flax and wild cotton that grew in some of these same lands.

Then those who raised goats and sheep discovered that the coats of these animals could also be spun and woven to make warm clothing and blankets, mats and rugs.

The wool from these early, half-wild animals was nothing so fine as we have today. It was coarse and hairy rather than fleecy, but it was a marvelous material even so. Best of all, it came with the seasons, like the grain. The heavy winter fleece could be shredded or cut away in the spring, and the valuable animal did not have to be killed to give its warm coat for the comfort of the farmer and his family. A man who owned a flock of goats or sheep had a great treasure.

Where sheep were herded, the dog took on a new job. Besides being an ideal hunting companion and camp guardian, he turned out to be a talented shepherd. He had to be taught, of course, not to kill the sheep. Men began to train dogs for these opposite tasks of hunting and sheep-herding, and eventually they developed separate breeds of hunting and herding dogs.

Like the dog, the cat may have adopted people instead of people adopting the cat. When men began to store their grain, rats and mice became serious pests to the farmers. But to the small wild cats that hunted these rodents, the grain stores were a happy hunting ground. Naturally the family made such a useful little animal welcome, and so cats took to living with men and earning their keep as protectors of the grain, earning affection as well for their beauty and charm.

In time the house cat became less a working member of

the household than a pampered pet, but it never lost its taste for hunting mice, rats, and other small marauders, and accordingly, it was highly honored. In ancient Egypt there was a law against killing a cat, and cats were sacred to the goddess Bubastis, who was also called Pasht. The pet terms "puss" and "pussy" came from her name. When a cat died in Egypt it was embalmed like a mummy, ceremoniously buried, and mourned like a member of the family.

Meanwhile other animals were coming to live with men. The cow came into men's new way of life first as a crop robber, feeding on the young grain the farmer had planted with so much toil and trampling what it did not eat. We can imagine the family's rage and despair when a herd of wild cattle got into the fields. The idea of domesticating them was a daring one. They were big beasts, bigger than sheep or goats and far fiercer. Not only the bulls but the cows, too, had dangerous horns. Perhaps the farmers began with the young ones, calves and heifers, which they somehow trapped away from the herd, and perhaps the mother cows followed their young ones and so were trapped with them. A full-grown wild bull would be nearly impossible to capture alive and unhurt, but a bull calf could be raised in captivity to become the father of a herd.

Once they succeeded in taming cattle, the farmers found that they had acquired a great care but also a great good. Slaughtering the large animals gave a quantity of meat and hides. The cows gave milk, and cattle could be tamed to carry burdens, pull a sledge or a plow, trample the grain on the threshing floor, turn a mill or a water wheel. A goat could be harnessed to carry or pull a light load but a bull had the strength of many men. Like the cats in Egypt, cows became sacred among some peoples, and the bull became a powerful symbol of fertility.

The pig also began its domestic life as a thief, rooting in the farmers' fields, and probably it was captured and tamed over and over again, because the wild boar is a very fierce beast and goes alone, and only the sow and piglets stay together as a family group. A sow and her litter would be easy to capture, and they would also be easy to care for. They could be penned in a sty and fed or they could be herded into the woods to find their own acorns, beechnuts, and whatever food was available, and they could be watched by children. Pigs were an excellent domestic animal because they produced two large litters of piglets every year, they gave quantities of meat and fat, and they would eat anything that could be eaten. Pigs were the town street cleaners from very ancient times until people stopped throwing their garbage into the streets, no more than about two hundred years ago.

People domesticated different kinds of animals in different parts of the world—water buffalo in India and Southeast Asia, llamas in the high Andes of South America. Some took to herding animals and never settled down. They kept sheep or goats and lived a wandering life, following their herds from pasture to pasture. Wandering peoples tamed horses on the plains and camels on the deserts. In Asia people domesticated elephants as work animals and beasts of burden, and in many parts of the world they captured wild asses and bred the donkey and the burro. In the far north people used the reindeer as their domestic animals, although they never really tamed the herds but only followed them. People also tried to tame the gazelle, but they were not successful with this fleet-footed, graceful little member of the antelope family.

But it was the farmers, and not the wandering herds-men, who were the men of the future. They settled down to live in villages, and this became the new way of life. It began in the same part of the world where the Neander-thal and the Cro-Magnon men had long been living in caves and hunting the big game. These were the ones who had not migrated to Europe but had stayed behind in the lands of the eastern Mediterranean. They had found the game plentiful, and they had made their homes in caves because caves were natural shelters from rain, storm, and dangerous animals. They had had ample time to develop good tools and hunting weapons, and they had made slow and steady progress in the arts of living. Unlike their rela-tives who had made the long trek to Europe and then stayed there through the Ice Age, these people had not faced any such fierce challenge to their lives until now, when the game disappeared.

Now their descendants, or people like them, showed their human talent for staying alive by skill and inventive-ness. When they took to planting crops and taming ani-mals, they invented two great new ideas of living. Instead of depending on nature to produce their food, they would produce it themselves. And instead of going hungry when nature failed them, they would store food in times of plenty for the times when it was scarce.

This was the great revolution, the end of hunting and food-gathering from the wild, and the beginning of men's conquest over nature to make their lives more secure. The first villages of the New Stone Age looked very different from anything we know today, but they were the first step toward our modern world.

New Ways

The first villages were clusters of round huts like bee-hives. They were built out of brush or reeds woven around supporting posts, and plastered on the outside with mud clay which dried hard in the sun and made a good, weatherproof shelter. This kind of building, called wattle and daub, is still good in mild climates because it is easy to build and easy to repair, although it is not very durable. Later the people learned to make bricks out of clay mixed with straw, which they hardened first in the sun and still later in kilns. For thousands of years, people built their houses round and domed, even with bricks, and plastered them over on the outside with clay mud. Some of these brick houses were so durable that a whole village of them survived to be uncovered on the island of Cyprus. They are more than seven thousand years old and yet enough of the house walls are still standing so that we can tell how they were built.

Of the wattle-and-daub houses of about ten thousand years ago, not much is left. A mound is usually the only sign that a human settlement was once there, and when the explorers dig into it they may be able to see the round outlines of the little houses and the pounded earth floors. Sometimes the house might be partly dug into the ground, with the upper part built up over it with reeds. Inside there were pallets of straw to sleep on, woven or skin rugs and coverlets, and the family's belongings. But there was at first no furniture. People sat on the ground to talk, eat, and do their work, and most of this they did outside, in front of the open door.

However simple the life of the village might seem to us, it was much more complicated than the life in the caves. The cave people had lived as a clan or tribe, and the men of the tribe had hunted together. The women shared the care of the children and the work of curing skins and stitching clothing, and they went food-gathering together for safety, or just for company. The hunting peoples had their skilled toolmakers and weapon makers, and their artists. They had their magic ceremonies and their magician or priest to lead them. They had a well-organized community.

But now there was much more work to do. There were the fields to be cleared, plowed, and planted, and the growing crops to be protected against wild animals and marauding birds like the crows. There were the herds to be taken out to pasture each day and brought home into pens and folds at night, and they, too, had to be guarded against the wild animals and kept from straying off and getting hurt, killed, or simply lost.

There were the harvest seasons and the slaughtering seasons, when all able-bodied members of the community had to share in the work. And even though they grew crops and kept animals, they still went hunting and food-gathering to fill out their food supplies in the seasons when nature was generous, as farmers still hunt deer, wild ducks and rabbits, and farmers' wives and their children still pick wild cooking greens and wild berries.

Life was safer now but it was not easier. There were no longer any weeks of leisure such as the hunters enjoyed, when the hunting had been good and there was plenty of meat stored in the cave. The people of the village worked every day from dawn to dark. There was work for the old people and work for the children. As soon as a boy was big enough to walk and carry a stick, he went along with the older boys to herd the pigs or goats, the sheep or cows. And little girls learned early to card and spin the wool, soak the reeds for baskets, tend the fire, watch over the cooking pot, and look after the babies and children that were still too young to help with the work.

Wherever human beings have lived, they have left the record of their lives in their rubbish, the used and broken things they have tossed away. For these times of long ago, before people had invented writing, the rubbish is our history book. In the rubbish of the early villages we read how the people lived there. And we read how in this new way of life, again, human beings were always inventing. Now they needed a great many new tools.

To cut the grain they invented a sickle. At first it was just a row of sharp flints set into the side of a stick, like a saw, but later they made a curved blade with one end set into a handle, such as we still use. Their first hoe was simply a bent stick cut from a forked branch, with one end as a handle and the other pointed for digging. Their first plow was simply one of these wooden hoes, or a hoe with a flint blade, pulled by a rope to dig a shallow trench for planting.

They still made their blades out of stone, flint when they could get it, but now their stone tools were very much improved. After chipping the edge, the toolmaker would grind it and polish it with a polishing stone and coarse sand until it had a fine smooth edge and was really sharp. They set their ax heads and sickle blades in handles made of antler or bone, and sometimes they carved the handles in the shape of animals. When modern explorers found these tools in the ancient villages, some of the flint sickles still had along their edges the sheen of the grasses they had been used to cut.

They invented spindles and looms for weaving and ovens for baking. They designed a hand mill for grinding the grain, a shallow stone or clay basin with an opening at one side, which we call a quern. The housewife would kneel on the floor in front of the quern and grind the grain by rolling a rounded grinding stone back and forth over it. Then she would push the ground grain, or flour, out at the open end into a dish or bowl she had placed there to collect it.

She stored her grain in a pit in the floor, plastered with

clay and sometimes lined with basketry to keep it dry. Before she ground it, she would parch it in the oven, like popping corn, and then soak it. It could be eaten this way in a kind of gruel, or it could be ground into flour and baked into bread on a flat stone. She had no yeast to make the bread rise, and so her bread was a flat loaf, like the bread of the Children of Israel in the Bible and the bread that is still eaten in Middle Eastern countries.

When the soaking grain stood too long and fermented, the housewives of that time learned to make beer. When milk turned sour, they made cheese. They made bags and bottles out of skins, and they wove baskets out of grasses and reeds. At first they still had no pots for cooking except the vessels of skin, which could not be put directly on the fire but only on hot stones, or else they cooked in hollowed stones.

Some of the people of this time went on working with stone and learned to make beautiful polished stoneware for cooking and storing foods, oil, and the medicines and cosmetics that little by little they learned to manufacture. But in other places the people experimented with making a new kind of pot. They plastered a basket with clay so that it could hold liquids, the way they plastered their wattle houses to keep out the rain. When they put these clay-covered baskets on the fire to cook, they found that the fire baked the clay hard. So they skipped the basket-making step and molded the pot directly out of clay.

That was a fine invention, the invention of pottery. Like the stone tools and weapons of the hunters, it was highly practical and at the same time it was an invitation to create beautiful objects. The potters became skillful craftsmen and artists. They created beautiful forms for even a simple water jug or a bowl, and they decorated their work with handsome designs and pictures of animals and people.

The invention of practical cooking pots of stone and clay made a great change in the people's diet. The cereal grains, hard to eat raw, could now be cooked into gruel or porridge. Tough meat could be softened by cooking it for a long time. Bones could be cooked down to make nourishing soup. This made for a much more economical use of food supplies.

And it had another, and quite surprising, result. More babies lived to grow up and more grownups lived to grow old. Babies and young children could eat porridge and soup before they could chew tough raw foods, or have it chewed for them, as they had had to do in the hunting life. And older people could still get good nourishment even after they had begun to lose their teeth.

The village life was easier for the children and the old people in other ways, too. They had a settled place to live and did not have to endure the long journeys when the tribe moved out of the camp or the cave to follow the game. There were fewer accidents than in the dangerous hunting life, and if someone was injured he could more easily be cared for until he recovered.

It was true that with more people living closely together, and living closely with animals as well, they began to catch more diseases. But at the same time it was much easier to take care of the sick.

A whole new magic grew up about sickness, which was

thought to come from evil spirits, or because someone was ill-wishing the sick person, or because he had done something wrong and was being punished.

The village priest, whom we would call a medicine man or witch doctor, had magic ways of dealing with these magic causes of sickness. He came dressed in a special costume, wearing a painted mask or with his face painted to look like a mask, and he carried a medicine bag of strange and mysterious objects—an animal's tooth or claw, a bone, a stone of a special shape, a scrap of fur or hair, a bit of bark, some dried herbs. Once he decided what had caused the sickness he began his cure. He danced, he chanted spells, and at the right moment he would put his hand on the place that was hurting and seem to draw out a stone or bone or something of the kind that was causing the pain.

He did this, of course, by a sleight-of-hand trick, just as modern-day magicians do. But he was not deceiving the people. They understood that their sickness was caused by magic, and so it took magic to cure it.

At the same time the priest-doctors used a great many real and practical medicines to help relieve the pain and cure the sickness. Even during the hunting days, men had experimented with all kinds of plants and herbs as medicines, and some of them are still good medicines today. They would give a man with a headache some willow bark to chew, or they would make a broth out of it for him to drink. And it did help his headache, because willow bark contains salicylic acid, which is what we take when we take aspirin.

They would roll a feverish patient in mud from the river bank to cool him, in the same way that we sponge the patient with alcohol. If we are out walking in the country and someone gets a bee sting, we quickly plaster mud on the bite—and so did these men of long ago.

The medicine men and the wise old women were the doctors of that time. They would roam the hillsides and the woods, picking all kinds of plants and natural substances to use in curing the sick. They used leaves, flowers, nuts, berries, roots, bark, ground-up earths and stones. Many of their substances were good medicine, like the willow bark. But they would also use many that were supposed to have magic power, such as bits of feather, fur, or some other part of an animal or a bird. The owl was a particularly magical bird, with its great eyes shining at night like a ghostly spirit and its mysterious hooting call like a spirit calling.

The medicine men and the wise women would gather their medicinal materials at certain special times, like the full moon or the dark of the moon, and at special places. They would keep all this very secret, too, because it was dangerous to deal with the unseen powers unless one had been carefully taught. They would hand their secrets on only to a son or daughter, or someone they considered worthy and able to carry on their dangerous work.

Nowadays we discard the magic and use only the medicine. We know that a medicine works not by magic but by its chemical ingredients. All the rest was belief and not fact. Those who believed in the magic may have been helped by their belief, but they were more effectively helped by the healing ingredients in the medicine man's strange mixtures.

The magician-doctors knew how to do certain kinds of surgery from a very early time. If a man had a really dreadful headache that would not go away, or if he had fits or behaved strangely, they understood that an evil spirit had got into his head, and they would cut an opening in his skull to let the spirit out. They did this so skillfully with their flint surgical knives that very often the patient recovered. Among the fossil remains that have been found, there are skulls that show how the operation was done, and also that it healed.

When a medicine or a treatment failed, and the patient died, there would always be a magic explanation for that, too. The people did not need to be told about the powerful forces that they could not see, forces that might be friendly and helpful at times, and at other times cruel and destructive. They could see these forces at work in their lives almost any day. The same rain that showered down gently, helping their crops to grow, could also come in a fierce flood and wash away all the tender seedlings. Their flocks and herds could be healthy one day, and the next day the animals might lie sick and dying from some mysterious illness.

And so this was a time when religion grew to great importance in the life of the people. The hunting peoples of the past had had religious rites for bringing success to the hunt, and they had also made little magic statues for the fertility of the game and of their women. Now fertility was the people's greatest need. They wanted their animals to bear many lambs, kids, and calves. They wanted their wives to give them many children who would grow up and help with the work. Most of all, they wanted the earth to be fertile and grow good crops, for their lives depended on the harvest.

They still made the little fertility statues of women, like those of the mammoth hunters long before. They had ceremonies to bring rain. They studied the moon and they planted and reaped according to whether it was waxing or waning, new or full. They prayed to the sun. At the winter solstice, when the days were short and the sunlight was weak, they lit great bonfires to revive the sun.

They celebrated the spring and the reawakening of the earth with special festivals. They sacrificed animals and they made human sacrifices, sprinkling the blood over the fields to bring the earth back to life and make it fertile. A great worship grew up, of a goddess of the earth, a mother goddess to whom they prayed and made sacrifices so that she would give life to the earth and bring them good harvests and good increases in their flocks and herds. People worshiped this goddess in many lands and under many different names. Thousands of years later, the ancient Greeks of Athens and Sparta still worshiped her, and one of their names for her was Ceres. It was her name that gave us our word cereal.

The people of the first villages did not only pray and sacrifice. They also worked very hard. Their labors brought forth good crops and good animals, and they were able to lay up good stores of grains and vegetables and gather large flocks and herds. People became prosperous. They lived longer and had more children, and more and more people came to live in settled communities. The villages grew until they became towns.

It seems that in the history of human beings, every new good brings with it some new evil. Now the evil was that when the people of a village did well, there were also others who did not do so well. The wandering tribes, those who did not settle down and cultivate the soil, were often hungry. When they were hungry they would raid the villages. They would take the farmers' stores of grain and drive off their flocks and herds. Often they burned the houses and killed the farmers who tried to defend their goods and their families.

Sometimes the attackers were not wandering tribesmen but the people of a nearby village, farmers like themselves, with whom they had some quarrel or feud. Feuds between neighbors can be bitter, and they can go on for a long time.

So the villagers found that they had to defend themselves. They built walls, and set guards around the walls. The oldest town we know was a walled town.

The Walls of Jericho

The story is told in the Bible of how the Children of Israel were led by Joshua out of the wilderness after Moses died there. They came to the walls of a town called Jericho, and when the people of the town proved unfriendly, Joshua commanded the Israelites to march around the town, blowing their ram's-horn trumpets. They did this every day for six days, and on the seventh day, after they had marched around seven times, Joshua commanded the people to shout. And, as the song says, the walls came tumbling down.

Jericho in the ancient Hebrew means "city of the Moon God." In the valley of the Jordan River, a few miles north of where it empties into the Dead Sea, there was a town in the time of the Crusades that was called Eriha, which may be the same name as Jericho, changed over the centuries and through many languages. A village of the same name still exists there, with the ruins of a Crusader castle. Not far from the village, on an oasis that is kept green by a never failing spring, explorers of our own century have dug out of the ground the ancient walled town of Jericho.

The town the diggers found was there even before the time of Joshua in the Bible story. It was first built about ten thousand years ago, by a people who had been living a hunting life in rock shelters on the hillsides nearby. They had been coming there to gather food and draw water from the spring for a long time before they settled on the oasis and began to live a village life.

At first they still hunted for most of their food and harvested the wild grains and other growing things to fill out their food supply. All that is left of that very early time is a place like a shrine, with a rough mud-plastered floor in which there are round hollows, like grain storage pits. The remains of the shrine show that it was burned, and perhaps the whole first village was raided and burned.

The village was destroyed and rebuilt more than once,

until at last the people built a town with a great stone wall around it, five feet thick. Around that they dug a ditch, twenty-eight feet wide and eight feet deep, cut out of solid limestone. Inside the wall they built a gigantic watchtower from which they could see the surrounding country and watch out for their enemy. The tower was of solid stone masonry, forty feet thick, and down through the center of it they built a stairway for the town sentinels to go up and down.

About thirty feet of the tower are still standing, and many steps of the stairway are still there. Each step is a single slab of stone three feet wide.

We can guess what labor it took to cut the great ditch and build the wall and the tower with its stairway. They had no steel picks like ours to break the rock, only stone hammers to pound it with. Far away from Jericho and thousands of years later, the Egyptians quarried out rock for their pyramids by setting a fire against the place where they wanted the rock to split, and then pouring water on it while it was hot. Repeated heating and chilling would eventually crack the rock enough so that they could drive in a wedge. Then they would hammer away, driving in thicker wedges all the time, until the stone that they wanted for building would split away. The people of Jericho must have used such a method to cut the rock from the ditch and build the fortifications of their town.

The wall enclosed a town of eight or ten acres, and it protected the town for a thousand years. Twice in that time the people rebuilt and added to the wall until it

stood sixteen feet high, and on top they laid still another
level built of bricks. They strengthened the tower as well,
both times, adding another and another layer of stonework
around the outside. Just inside the wall they kept a water
supply in a row of tanks made of mud bricks covered with
plaster. A channel from the top of the tower led the rain-
water into the tanks.

The people who did this heroic labor to defend their
town were small and slender, not much above five feet tall.
They built their houses of the same round-topped bricks
they put on their wall, and the houses were round or oval,
with a dome-shaped roof of wattle and clay. Some of the
houses had only one room, but some were quite grand
three-room dwellings. The floors and walls were plastered
with mud clay, and the floors were sunk below the level of
the outside ground, with wooden steps leading down into
the rooms through doorways with wooden doorposts.
There were no streets in the town—people went to and fro
by way of courtyards and little alleys between the houses.

These people brought with them from their early life in
the rock shelters a curious custom of burying their dead
under the place where they lived. Burials were in graves
three or four feet under the house floor. Sometimes, after
the master died, the family pulled the whole house down
and built another one to live in.

After a thousand years, Jericho's defenses failed and a
new people came to live within its walls—perhaps the same
people against whom the walls had been built in the first
place. They built a new kind of house, not round and

domed but rectangular, as we have been building our houses ever since. Their houses had several rooms connected by wide doorways, and they were built of brick on stone foundations. The walls and floors were covered not with mud clay but with fine plaster, which they colored red or pinkish with ocherous earth and polished smooth. They were the first of the farmer folk who took some trouble over interior decoration, and they had mats of rushes, some round and some rectangular, on their polished floors.

The new people of Jericho still did not make pottery, but they were skillful in making vessels out of stone. The town was built on limestone—fairly soft stone as stone goes, often with beautiful markings and veinings. To make a bowl or a pot, the craftsman would chop out a piece of the right size and then chip a hollow in the center of it with a stone pick or chisel. Then he would enlarge the hollow and slowly, patiently grind it and polish it with stone powder. The result was often a very beautiful bowl, with sides as thin as fine pottery or china.

The craftsmen of Jericho also made the mother-goddess statuettes like the people who had lived there before them, and they also buried their dead under the floors of their houses. But they had another custom that seems even stranger to us. They saved the skull and covered it over with plaster, and on the plaster they modeled and painted a portrait of the dead person, with small shells set in for the eyes. They kept these skull portraits in the house as a memorial and perhaps they prayed to it, as people in many lands have prayed to their ancestors.

From these portraits we have a very good idea of what the people looked like. They had long heads, high foreheads and rather small faces, with fine, delicate features—straight nose, small mouth, small pointed chin. Most of the faces are clean-shaven, but on one there are still the painted traces of a mustache.

When Jericho was most prosperous, as many as two or three thousand people lived within its walls. The men and women went out every day to till the fields outside the walls, and the children to pasture the animals. Theirs was a large population to be living together in one settlement. Jericho is the oldest town, and the only walled and fortified town that we know of in that time.

Villages, Towns, Cities

By seven or eight thousand years ago, there were other large settlements. People had discovered that it was good for a number of people to live close together. They could divide the work of farming and animal care, and some among them could develop special skills like toolmaking, stone working, and pottery, and work at these crafts full time because they benefitted everybody. Now that they were producing and storing their food, there was enough to support people who worked at other tasks.

Villages as big as towns grew up in many places around the eastern Mediterranean. One was on the island of Cyprus, just south of the peninsula of Anatolia, at a place called Khirokitia. This was a huge settlement of about a thousand houses that spread over the top of a hill, in the curve of a winding river. The houses, built of brick, were round and domed and plastered over with clay in the old style. Inside, however, they had a second story like a balcony, built out halfway over the main room, where the family climbed up to sleep. Khirokitia must have been a pleasant place to live, fertile and green through the long Mediterranean summer.

Khirokitia was a large village and Jericho was a walled town, but high on the fertile plain of Anatolia there was a town that was more like a small city. The place where its ruins have been found is called Çatal Hüyük and it covers thirty-two acres, compared with Jericho's eight or ten. It is at least eighty-five hundred years old—possibly older—and it lasted for about eight hundred years.

There was no wall around Çatal Hüyük, but the houses were built in a most ingenious way for defense against an enemy. Each house was a group of rooms, usually one or more main rooms for living, surrounded by many small storerooms and with a courtyard in the center. The plan of such a house was like many rectangular blocks of different sizes put together in an irregular way so that the outside walls went around many corners and angles. What is ingenious about the houses is that they had no doors at all in their outer walls, and only very small windows placed very high up. The way into the house was down through a hole in the roof into the main room. From this room there were only little low doorways into all the other rooms, some less than two and one-half feet high, which one had to go through crouching or even crawling.

The houses were built up against one another and on different levels, some higher and some lower. One would climb up and down ladders and over the roofs of the neighbors to visit a friend. If an enemy were to break through the wall of one of the houses on the edge of the town, he would not be likely to get very much farther. He would be trapped in the rooms below, and the defenders would be waiting for him on the roof. In that part of the world houses have been built this way up to quite recent times for protection against floods as well as enemies.

The houses were built of brick with a wooden framework, and overhead there were sturdy wooden roof beams holding up a heavy three-layered roof. The central layer was a reed thatch, on top was a thick layer of mud clay, (sun-baked to the hardness of a pavement), and under the reeds there was a tightly woven mat to keep litter from the thatch from drifting down into the room below.

We discover that built-in furniture, which is so much a part of modern interior design, is actually older than movable furniture. These houses had all their furniture built into and against the walls. They had benches built in, and platforms like sofas or divans which were actually beds. The master of the house had his sleeping platform, the wife had hers, and there were small ones for the children. There was a built-in recess for storing the wood, brush, and straw for the fire, and there were niches in the walls for oil lamps made of stone. Daylight and air came in from the roof entrance and the small high windows, and smoke from the hearth and the lamps went out the same way.

In the storerooms there were clay grain bins three or four feet high, which were filled from the top but emptied through a small opening in the bottom, so that the grain that had been stored longest and was most subject to spoiling would be used first. There were clay boxes in rows, holding ax heads, polishing stones, extra supplies of tools, and articles for household use. Querns and mortars for grinding the grain were sunk into the floor.

The people of Catal Hüyük raised as many as fourteen different food plants. They had barley and several varieties of wheat, lentils, peas, and other legumes, and they either grew or brought from the hills apples, pistachio nuts, almonds, and berries. They made beer, and out of one kind of berry, the hackberry, they made wine.

They were skilled weavers who made not only rush and grass mats but rugs and cloth for clothing out of sheep's and goat's wool. They dyed their cloth and rug yarns with vegetable dyes from plants that grew in their region and gave rich reds, blues, yellows, and other colors. They wove patterns in their rugs that are still used by weavers of that district.

They made beautiful wooden ware—bowls, dishes, cups, huge meat platters, boxes of various shapes with well-fitted

Jericho, the oldest known town where people began to live together about 10,000 years ago, had a great wall and a round watchtower which may have looked like this.

lids. They had very little flint, but the nearby mountains gave them greenstone which made good ax heads, and a black or brownish volcanic glass called obsidian, out of which they made excellent tools and weapons and even mirrors, highly polished and without a scratch. They imported marble and beautiful semiprecious stones—rock crystal, malachite, carnelian, jasper, chalcedony—out of which they made ornaments and jewelry. They knew how to pierce the tiniest of holes in a little stone bead without breaking it, in order to string it.

And they had discovered metal. The mountains that ringed their plain were full of lead and copper ore, and these people had learned how to smelt it. Copper and lead are soft metals, and they had not yet discovered how to blend metals to make a hard alloy such as bronze, which is an alloy of copper and tin. So their metals were not suitable for blades or sharp tools, and they still used stone for their knives and axes, their hunting weapons and farm tools. But they used their metals for beautiful objects, beads and finger rings and settings for semiprecious stones in a brooch or pin.

The women and even the children wore necklaces, bracelets, anklets, rings. The women had decorative brooches to fasten their dresses and the men had decorative buckles for their belts and splendid stone-bladed daggers with carved bone handles. One was found with a handle carved in the shape of a coiled serpent, complete with scales and beady eyes, and a fine twine is wound smoothly and elegantly over the joining of handle and blade.

There was plenty of food from the fields, and there were
herds of sheep and goats, but the men still hunted, perhaps
as much for pleasure as for meat. They hunted deer, wild
asses, wild oxen, boars, and leopards. Leopard skin was a
fashionable article of clothing, and warm in the chilly
winter months in Anatolia, where there is often snow. The
women wore a shift or robe fastened at the shoulder, and
the men a loincloth with a cloak or tunic over it. Fringe
was a decoration they liked, and one young girl's skirt has
been found that is made entirely of string fringe, with tiny
copper tubes fastened as weights around the bottom ends
of the fringe.

The men had excellent stone spearheads and arrowheads
for hunting, and they wore wrist guards made of bone to
protect their forearms against the snap of the bowstring.
They had maces, a weapon like a club with a stone head,
and they had another new weapon, the slingshot, for which
they made special ammunition, little pellets of hard-baked
clay. The men carried flint firestones to make fire, and
some ingenious craftsmen among them invented a combi-
nation tool of firestone, knife, and scraper, a Stone Age
equivalent of a pocketknife with attachments.

The women had bone ladles to serve up a soup or a
stew, and little bone spoons and spatulas with which to
feed their young children. They had awls and bodkins for
sewing and mending. And they had whole cosmetic sets—
shells containing ocher, little baskets of rouge already
mixed out of red ocher and animal fat, ointment sticks, a
palette to mix their cosmetics on, and a spoon and a small
fork to mix them with.

Besides all their excellent crafts, these people had an art of painting and sculpture that we have not seen since the cave art of the hunters, thousands of years before. They had wall paintings of hunting scenes, and one picture that shows their town with its smoking volcano—the volcano is still there but it is no longer active. But mostly their paintings and statues were devoted to the great mother goddess of fertility. They showed her standing, kneeling, sitting on a throne, giving birth. They showed her with leopard cubs, and most of all with bulls and bulls' heads. They surrounded her with decorative designs of flowers, stars, insects, and butterflies. And they had many pictures and even whole painted borders of human hands.

Most of the paintings and sculptures were in the shrines, fine buildings where they also stored the town supplies of grain. But they also painted panels and posts in their houses, and in every house there was a carved or painted bull's head on a wall, an object of veneration and a protection for the prosperity of the house.

The people kept their houses scrupulously clean. They used the courtyard as a dumping place for their rubbish and probably also as their toilet, but this, too, was kept tidy and sanitary, covered over against odors and unpleasantness with the ashes of their hearth fires, which acted as a sterilizer. Each year after the spring rains they replastered their houses inside and outside. From the number of coats of plaster we can tell that some of the houses were lived in for more than a hundred years, until the walls leaned and the plaster bulged and the people tore the house down and built a new one over the rubble. Fire was a constant danger, and once at least the entire city burned and was rebuilt.

So much care and living comfort, so much luxury and adornment tell us that farming had become a most prosperous way of life. It could support not only villages and towns but cities as well. In a village everyone works at farming, in a town nearly everyone, but in a city only a small part of the population can produce enough food for all.

A city can afford full-time craftsmen, tradesmen, priests, overseers, managers, governors. Cities have more than enough for their own people's needs and can trade and barter. They can import raw materials and export manufactured goods. Çatal Hüyük was a forecast of the future way of life, the life of cities.

Time Moves Faster

Trade was now spreading the new way of life. Good stone for tools was becoming rare, and it was one of the first articles of trade. All through the eastern Mediterranean lands, from Asia to European Turkey and Greece and the islands, traders were going to and fro, bartering raw stone and finished stone tools. With trade, knowledge spread, and people learned more and more swiftly about new inventions and new and better ways of doing things.

Northern Europe still knew little of these new arts and

ways. In northern Europe even five thousand years ago, vast forests still covered the land, and men still lived in small, isolated settlements on the edges of lakes and marshes, widely separated and without much knowledge of each other. They were still hunting and fishing and gathering wild foods. But up from the south, along the valley of the Danube River, farmers from the Mediterranean countries began to move northward in search of new farmlands.

In the north the farmers had to clear forests before they could plant, and they developed the arts of lumbering and woodcraft. With plentiful supplies of wood, they built log houses and wooden boats and they learned to make charcoal for slow, long-burning fires. Their axes and woodworking tools had to be good, and now in northern Europe, too, the stone for tools became an article of trade. Flint mines began to be worked in Poland, Denmark, Sweden, France, Belgium, and Britain, and it was traded over wide localities. A certain kind of reddish-yellow flint from France was especially good for knives and sickles. Other flints made the best ax heads, and some of the workshops were specialized ax factories.

Those first miners chipped and hammered the flint out of the chalk and rock beds where it was found, using picks made of deer antler. They used the heavy end for a handle, and hacked off all the tines except the heaviest one, the "brow," which they sharpened to a point. To shovel away the debris, they used the shoulder blade of an ox, and they carried the flint they had dug in baskets on their backs.

Sometimes the stone had to be carried long distances to the workshops.

The ax heads of this time were of very fine quality, ground and polished with sand and special polishing stones. Quite recently some Danish scientists experimented with ax heads of this time from the Copenhagen Museum, fitting them with wooden handles like the original ones. Three men using these axes cut down nearly three and one-half acres of birch forest in four hours, and one four-thousand-year-old ax was used to chop down more than a hundred trees without having to be sharpened. The modern woodchoppers found that the ancient stone axes had to be used with a short swinging motion from the elbow instead of a full-armed swing from the shoulders as a steel ax is used today.

Even with efficient axes, clearing the great oak forests was the heaviest kind of labor. After the trees were felled, there were still the stumps and roots to be chopped out of the ground before it could be planted. These early farmers took to saving their axes and their muscle by burning the trees down. This gave them good soil for a while, but weeds and brush would grow again which their primitive hoes could not dig out, and so they would move on and burn another clearing in the forest and plant fresh fields.

This was a wasteful way to use the land, but it is still done in many parts of the world. In Europe, after thousands of years, the people learned at last to conserve their woodlands and cultivate their farmlands more efficiently.

All this time the people were developing new crops and

new breeds of animals. When they first began to harvest
the wild grains, they found that in some varieties the ripe
heads would burst open at a touch and the seeds would
scatter far and wide so that they could not be gathered. So
the gatherers would look for the grasses whose heads held
firm while they were cut and carried home where the
grain seeds could be threshed out on a clean floor. When
they began to plant crops, the farmers chose the better
seeds; and so by careful selection the grains were steadily
improved.

The farmers did the same with their other crops—the
peas, beans, and lentils, the green and root vegetables, the
olive and fruit trees that they planted in orchards, and the
wild grapes that they brought in to cultivate in vineyards.

The animals, too, steadily improved. The wild breeds
with which the farmers began were thin and rangy, easily
frightened, fierce when cornered, difficult to herd and care
for. Little by little they changed. The animals that were
born and bred on the farm and accustomed to being fed
became gentler and easier to manage. Their bodies
changed, and even their size. Now that they no longer had
to get their own food and protect themselves from their
enemies in the wild, they became smaller, with lighter
bones and heavier, plumper flesh. Their coarse, hairy coats
became sleek, and the sheep and some kinds of goats grew
coats of soft fleece or mohair that made the finest weaving
yarns. Cattle were developed into different breeds, some
for milk, some for beef, and some for work. Pigs grew
fatter and fatter.

From Asia and Africa across the Mediterranean to Europe came the first grains and vegetables, most of the fruit trees, the olive trees and grapevines, the flax for linen and linseed oil, and the cotton for cotton cloth. From these parts of the world also came the first kinds of domesticated animals, and from India came rice, and later the first chickens, tamed from a kind of jungle fowl that still roams wild there.

It was about eight thousand years ago that some of these farmers began to migrate into Europe from Asia, and a little later from northern Africa, bringing seeds and breeding animals and the arts of cultivation, just as the colonists a few hundred years ago came to America with field and garden seeds, young trees, and young animals.

In the New World to which the Europeans first came five hundred years ago, men had long been growing crops and taming animals, but they were different crops and different animals. Here men grew corn, which the Europeans called maize, and as long as six thousand years ago in Mexico they had already developed new varieties of corn that were better than the wild. Here men had also domesticated fruits and vegetables that were wonderfully strange to the explorers from Spain. The Spaniards took back to Europe potatoes and sweet potatoes, tomatoes, peppers both sweet and hot, squash, and chocolate.

Since then men have continued to develop new and better varieties of crops and breeds of animals, and they have continued to learn and borrow from each other. They have brought out of the woods and wilds not only foods, and animals for food, but trees and shrubs and garden flowers to cultivate just for their beauty, and some animals to keep and love just for their company. And more and more people are living, like the people of Çatal Hüyük, in cities.

It is hard to believe that all this began when people looked around at the end of the Ice Age, ten thousand years ago, and saw that they had to get their living in some other way than hunting, the only way of life they had known for perhaps a million years. And that in the next three or four thousand years they had already learned to build villages, towns, and cities, and to live with so much more comfort, security, and grace.

All this they had accomplished while they still had nothing more than stone for their tools and only word of mouth for their communication. Their greatest invention was still to come, the invention of writing.

For the world of six thousand years ago, writing was just over the horizon, five hundred years in the future. With it would come the beginning of history. And so this is the end of the prehistoric world of man, and the end of our own adventure into our Ice Age past.

Human evolution was a continuous process, but only major developments are shown in this chronology. Shaded areas indicate large periods of time. The chart shows that Cro-Magnon men appeared during the long Neanderthal period. The two races then existed concurrently, and both disappeared around the same time.

YEARS AGO	ICE AGE	STONE AGE	HUMAN EVOLUTION
5,000		NEW STONE AGE	Jericho—first village
10,000		MIDDLE STONE AGE	Jericho—first town
15,000			Magdalenians
20,000	FOURTH ICE AGE		mammoth hunters (Gravettians)
25,000			
30,000			
35,000			
40,000			CRO-MAGNON MEN
50,000			
75,000		OLD STONE AGE	NEANDERTHAL MEN
100,000	THIRD INTERGLACIAL PERIOD		
	THIRD ICE AGE		
200,000			
300,000	SECOND INTERGLACIAL PERIOD		
400,000			
	SECOND ICE AGE		PITHECANTHROPUS
500,000	FIRST INTERGLACIAL PERIOD		
600,000	FIRST ICE AGE		
700,000			
1,000,000			
			AUSTRALOPITHECUS
5,000,000			

Index